BERLITZ®

INDIA

1991/1992 Edition

By the staff of Berlitz Guides

How to use our guide

These 256 pages cover the **highlights** of India, grouped into five regions. Although not exhaustive, our selection of sights will enable you to make the best of your trip.

The **sights** to see are contained between pages 59 and 191. Those most highly recommended are pinpointed by the Berlitz traveller symbol.

For **general background** see the sections India and the Indians (p. 8), Facts and Figures (p. 19), History (p. 20) and Religions of India (p. 50).

Entertainment and **activities** (including eating out) are described between pages 192 and 217.

The **practical information,** hints and tips you will need before and during your trip begin on page 218. This section is arranged alphabetically with a list for easy reference.

The **map section** at the back of the book (pp. 244–252) will help you find your way around and locate the principal sights.

Finally, if there is anything you cannot find, look in the complete **index** (pp. 253–256).

Text: Jack Altman
Staff Editor: Christina Jackson
Photography: Walter Imber
Layout: Doris Haldemann
Cartography: Falk-Verlag, Hamburg

Library of Congress Catalog Card No. 85-814 52

5th Printing
1991/1992 Edition
Updated or revised 1991, 1988

CONTENTS

CONTENTS

CONTENTS

Although we make every effort to ensure the accuracy of all the information in this book, changes occur incessantly. We cannot therefore take responsibility for facts, prices, addresses and circumstances in general that are constantly subject to alteration. Our guides are updated on a regular basis as we reprint, and we are always grateful to readers who let us know of any errors, changes or serious omissions they come across.

Acknowledgements
We wish to express our warmest thanks to the Government of India Tourist Office, in particular K. B. Singh, Asha Malhotra and Kamla Bhatnagar, as well as Air India and Indian Airlines, for their help in the preparation of this guide. We are also grateful to Kim Gordon-Bates, Adrienne Jackson, Afzal Friese, Vinita Schürch and Arun Pabari for invaluable assistance.

Cover photo: Taj Mahal by moonlight

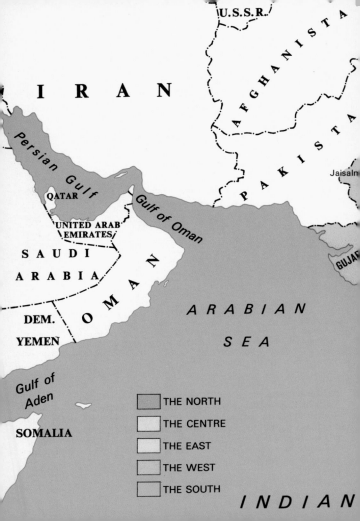

INDIA AND THE INDIANS

This land is a constant challenge to mind and body, a glorious shock to the system, no place for the faint-hearted. It's exhilarating, exhausting, delightful and infuriating. And you'll find the harsh, but equally often cheerful, practicalities of daily life overlay the fantasies and mysteries that the popular imagination has attached to the idea of India.

In place of the much touted, much misunderstood mysticisms of its ancient religions, the reality of India has quite another magic to offer, in the sheer profusion of its peoples and landscapes.

There *is* one India. It derives strength in part from a certain unifying geometry in that diamond-

shaped subcontinent stretching over 3,000 kilometres (1,800 mi.) north-south from the mountains of Kashmir down to the southern-most tip at Cape Comorin on the Indian Ocean. East-west, it spans another 3,000 kilometres from Arunachal Pradesh and Assam on the border with China and Burma to the Gujarat coast on the Arabian Sea. That's the political reality. Only in the recent post-colonial era did it exclude from the subcontinent's natural geography the now separate countries of Pakistan and Bangladesh. Even there, for all the perennial hostilities, there's an undeniable cultural affinity with In-

A whole world separates Bihari rice-workers from this Rajasthani camel-boy, but India unites them.

dia—feuding brothers rather than unrelated strangers.

In fact, when we look at its 4,000 years of history—or today's newspapers, for that matter—feuds seem to be a necessary and perpetual dynamic of Indian civilization. It's a very big family, with a lot of different and inevitably conflicting regional and sectarian interests. Pick up a rupee banknote and you'll see the sum of money printed in India's 15 state-recognized languages (in addition to English)*. A recent count of the languages actually being spoken all over the country, leaving out the dialects, came up with the modest figure of 1,652, written in 13 different alphabets.

The national language, Hindi, is still spoken by less than a majority of the population. English, for which the government conducts a permanent campaign as part of its programme of modernization, is spoken by only 3 per cent of the people, nearly all of them in the major cities. (But everybody "speaks" the national sport of cricket with the jargon of *innings, wickets* and *boundaries* littering every dialect.)

One of the first impressions you'll get at the airport in Delhi or Bombay is the enormous diversity of ethnic types. From the light-complexioned, even blue-eyed and occasionally red-haired Kashmiris and the Chinese-Tibetan types from Sikkim or Darjeeling, through all the shades of coffee of the heartland, to dark-skinned, often curly-haired, Dravidians from southern India, you soon realize there's no such thing as a "typical" Indian.

India's earliest, prehistoric settlers were probably what anthropologists call Proto-Australoids. They've since been joined by a succession of Mongols, Aryans, Greeks, Arabs, Turks, Persians and Afghans, while Portuguese, French, Dutch and British have also left their traces.

The landscape is no less diverse, alternately rich and arid, lush and grim. On the northern frontier, the majestic snow-bound Himalayas make an appropriate home for the Hindu gods. Kashmir is a serenely beautiful and understandably coveted land of forest, alpine meadows and lakes, while the Punjab on the north-west is the fertile centre of the country's Green Revolution, helping to make the nation self-sufficient in wheat, barley and millet. But immediately adjacent, the Thar Desert of noble Rajasthan heralds the

---

*Hindi, Sanskrit, Sindhi, Urdu, Bengali, Marathi, Gujarati, Oriya, Punjabi, Assamese, Kashmiri, Telugu, Tamil, Malayalam, Kannada.

The Jain faith is as intricate as the maze of pillars in this temple on Mount Abu.

vast Deccan plateau of parched ruddy granite that dominates the peninsula of southern India.

Delhi stands at the western end of the Ganga* river basin in which the nation grows much of its rice. Flanked on its north by the occasional forest leading into the foothills of the Himalayas, the plain is flat right across to the Bay of Bengal, 1,600 kilometres (1,000 mi.) away. Several of the forests are kept as nature reserves to protect the country's wildlife, most notably the tiger, leopard and elephant. Bengal's greenery provides a threshold to the tea-plantations of Darjeeling to the north and Assam to the east.

The rugged plateau of the southern peninsula is hemmed in by a triangle of relatively low-lying mountain ranges—the Vindhya and Satpura to the north and the Western and Eastern Ghats running parallel to the coasts. But the Malabar coast on the west is rich in forest, with crops of coconut, betelnut, pepper, rubber and cashewnut still tempting merchant ships across the Arabian Sea. And some of the palm trees just serve to provide shade for sandy beach-resorts in Goa and Kerala.

The landscape is also man-made, and magnificently so. The

*Place-names have been "re-Indianized" since Independence: Ganga (Ganges), Pune (Poona), Kanpur (Cawnpore), Varanasi (Benares).

architectural treasures bear witness to the great religions and secular civilizations that have enriched the country, monuments at last preserved by the restoration programme of the Archaeological Survey of India after centuries of neglect.

Once again, the variety is endless: the gigantic Hindu *gopuram* tower-gates of the south, the temples of the holy city of Varanasi (Benares) and the astounding Buddhist cave-monasteries of Ajanta and Ellora, the beautiful erotic sculptures of Khajuraho, the splendid marble palaces, fortresses and mausoleums of the Mughal emperors and maharajas in Delhi, Agra and Rajasthan, but also the British Empire's grandiose government buildings in New Delhi or its bizarre Gothic-Oriental Victoria railway terminus in Bombay.

The big cities' shanty-town districts are often to be found squatting in the shadow of the shining new skyscrapers their residents have been hired to build—with the women most often carrying the loads of bricks on their heads as gracefully as a pitcher of water. The women are also responsible for one other characteristic element of Indian "architecture" —the cow-dung patties preserved for fuel and artfully shaped into temple-like mounds that differ in form from region to region, resembling a Buddhist stupa,

Hindu *gopuram* or even Moslem minaret.

The one constant of the landscape is the people themselves. They really are everywhere. Even in the vast open spaces of the Rajasthan desert or the Deccan plateau of central India, figures pop up from nowhere, a red-turbaned tribesman on camelback or lone woman holding the veil of her headdress in her teeth to keep out the dust as she carries on her head a huge clay pitcher of water or stack of firewood. If, as the road stretches before you clear to the horizon, you can see only one tree, it's a pretty safe bet you'll find at least one half-naked *sadhu* (holy man) resting in its shade.

The teeming millions of Calcutta and Bombay have of course become legendary. They crowd each other into the roadway, bulge out of tiny auto-rickshaws and perch on top of buses and trains; a family of four, even five, cling onto a motor-scooter, and what looks like a whole school-class on one bullock-cart. It's hazardous, buses do topple over, rooftop passengers on trains do occasionally get swept off by an overhanging steel rod, but they accept the risk for the free ride—rooftoppers don't buy tickets.

You'll soon notice the special genius Indians have acquired in these conditions for filling every available space—everyone learns to sit when necessary on just one buttock. It's a useful knack to acquire if you venture out in a bus or train, and you quickly learn to accept, not just the sight of so many people all around you, but also their touch, their smell, and their many and unabashed snorts and belches. It's important not to apply Western values to everything you see. The poverty, for instance, not creating a sense of shame as in so many Western countries, is borne with considerable dignity and even cheerfulness that some may find difficult to understand. So, too, jostling is a whole way of life.

But everyone makes way for the cow, as sacred to the Hindus as the pig is abhorred by Moslems or Jews. The cow has right of way everywhere, walking nonchalantly through the centre of the biggest cities, reclining across the new expressway between Lucknow and Delhi. After a while you begin to detect something other-worldly about the way the cow seems to look beyond its immediate surroundings—she *knows* she's sacred.

You can't get around it, India is a place where religion is ever present. Anthropologists, theologians, historians, thinkers on all sides, each has a pet explanation. The answer is enormously complex but one factor is almost certainly, quite simply, the weather. India just seems to have

13

more of it. The heat at its most intense, particularly from April to mid-June, can try the limits of human endurance, even among the Indians themselves. The equally powerful rains of the monsoon (normally from mid-June to September) are celebrated as a blessing when they come— but they don't always come, or they come too late, too little or too much. The disaster of flood or drought is perennial. In the temperate times between rains and heat (the season for conquerors or tourists), the sages of India no doubt ponder the meanings of those extremes.

Hinduism, embracing over 83 per cent of the population, is much more a way of life than a religion. The sacred ritual and observances are only a part of what good Hindus consider makes them good Hindus. Much more than the mystical and esoteric elements which have fascinated so many Westerners, Hinduism concerns itself with the nuts and bolts of everyday life: birth, health, work and social relationships, helped along by regular consultations with the local astrologer—by industrialists

How many incarnations have this family known to achieve such wistful melancholy?

and goat-herds alike—and a very easy-going attitude to one or more of the literally millions of gods in the Hindu pantheon, cursing or worshipful according to how well things are going.

The intricate Hindu caste-system, despite the many anti-discrimination statutes passed since Independence, still governs for most Indians their choice of job, spouse, even friends and, now-adays, political party. Brahmans,

Calcutta's millions are always on the move, but there's not enough room to hurry.

members of the priestly caste, fill many of the top posts in the universities and administration; many Indian Army officers trace their ancestry to the proud *kshatriya* warrior-caste; business is dominated by the merchant or

prestigious newspapers mention "caste no bar", just as many do specify the required caste or insist on a "fair-complexioned" bride, while touting perhaps the advertiser's university diploma and an American work-permit.

Over 80 million Moslems make up the second-largest religious group in India, almost as many as the whole population of the Islamic state of Pakistan. Most of them are descendants of Hindu converts from the time of the Mughals' Indian empire and have had to bear the brunt of Hindu retaliation for the years of subjection and a too close, if often unfair, identification with British rule prior to Independence.

Left behind by the massive exodus to Pakistan at the 1947 partition, they form a large part of the impoverished peasantry in the north, especially in the states of Uttar Pradesh and Bihar. While in general they prefer to keep a low profile in the larger cities, you will often hear of "communal incidents" involving fights between Hindus and Moslems on the pretext of some religious insult by one or other of the two communities.

Sikhs, combining in their faith elements of both Hinduism and Islam, are prominent in India out of all proportion to their numbers, just 2 per cent of the population. Part of this comes, of course, from the high visibility of their

vaishya caste; and *shudras* till the land. Untouchables have greater opportunities now to rise in the social scale, a few of them becoming captains of industry or cabinet ministers, but it's still their brethren who sweep the streets.

Most marriages are still arranged with carefully negotiated dowries. But if more and more matrimonial advertisements in the weekend editions of *The Times of India* and other equally

17

religious obligation to wear a beard and turban. They seem to drive most of the taxis in Delhi and, for some never satisfactorily explained reason, provide the country's most talented mechanics. Following a tradition created by their militant need to defend their faith, they make up a fiercely competent élite in the Indian Army. But they are also skilled farmers at the spearhead of the Green Revolution in the Punjab where most of them live. Their economic and political rights in the Punjab have been the source of perennial conflicts with the central government.

Indian Christians, a few descended from the Syrian community that came to India in the earliest days of Christianity, but mostly from converts by Portuguese or British missionaries, number about 19 million.

In the land of its birth, Buddhism practically disappeared in India after the invasions of the 7th century, but it has made a considerable comeback in recent years because of its appeal to Untouchables as an escape from Hindu discrimination. There are now more than 5 million, many of them in the western state of Maharashtra.

Two other religious minorities attract attention because of their prominence in the business world. The Jains' non-violent faith was founded around the same time as Buddhism and it excludes them from practising agriculture—but they now dominate, for instance, the electronics industry in Bangalore. The tiny but economically powerful community of Parsis brought their Zoroastrianism from Iran in the 8th century and shine today in the business world of Bombay.

But the new religion of India is Modernization. These days, Young Upwardly Mobile Professionals are everywhere. You'll see them waiting in the airport lounges with their three-piece suits (whatever the temperature) and black fibreglass attaché cases, the darlings of Prime Minister Rajiv Gandhi's "computer boys". India's growing involvement in electronics, telecommunications, nuclear power and space satellites is the new reality intended to take India, as one government official put it, "directly from the 19th into the 21st century".

To make this imaginative leap, the government is trying valiantly to cut through the notorious tangle of the bureaucracy, break with political corruption, find some kind of peaceful *modus vivendi* for communal and regional interests, and all within a sorely tried democratic framework. Former U.S. ambassador John Kenneth Galbraith called it a "functioning anarchy". The miracle of how it functions is well worth watching.

FACTS AND FIGURES

Geography: India's area of 3,287,593 square kilometres (1,269,246 sq. mi.) makes it the 7th largest country in the world. It stretches 3,220 kilometres (2,012 mi.) from Kashmir south to Cape Comorin on the Indian Ocean, and 2,980 kilometres (1,848 mi.) from the eastern frontier with China and Burma to the Gujarat coast on the Arabian Sea. The Himalayas mark the northern frontier, leading down to the vast plain of the Ganga river stretching east to the Bay of Bengal. In the north-east, Cherrapunji holds the record for the world's heaviest rainfall in a single year, 22,990 millimetres (905 inches) in 1861. The triangular Deccan plateau of the southern peninsula is bounded by the Vindhya and Satpura mountains to the north and the Eastern and Western Ghats running parallel to the Coromandel and Malabar coasts. Highest mountain: Kanchenjunga (Sikkim) 8,586 metres (28,168 ft.).

Population: 800 million of whom 72% are Indo-Aryan, mostly in north, 25% Dravidian in south, 3% others. Density is 232 people per square kilometre (500 per sq. mi.).

Capital: Delhi (pop. 6,420,000).

Major cities: Calcutta (10,052,000), Bombay (9,174,000), Madras (4,774,000), Bangalore (3,252,000), Ahmedabad (2,836,000), Hyderabad (2,833,000), Pune (1,876,000), Kanpur (1,824,000).

Government: India is a republic of 22 states, with 8 union territories governed from Delhi. A member of the Commonwealth, it has parliamentary government established by the 1950 constitution. The President has limited executive responsibility, real power being vested in a Prime Minister and Council of Ministers responsible to the 544 members of the Lok Sabha (House of the People). State government is in the hands of Chief Ministers and state legislatures, represented centrally by a 244-member Rajya Sabha (Council of States).

Religion: 83% Hindu, 11% Moslem, 2.5% Christian, 2% Sikh, 1.5% Buddhist, Jain and others.

HISTORY

India has always been a hodge-podge of peoples from all over the place.

Apart from some traces of pre-Ice Age hominids, the first settlers were Negritos and Proto-Austra-loids, ancestors of today's tribal peoples in central India. Migrants of Mediterranean stock coming overland from the Middle East and others from central Asia seem to have made up the Dravidians, now principally in the southern peninsula, who speak a language entirely separate from the Indo-European languages of the north.

In 4000 B.C., neolithic agricul-turalists made their first appear-ance up in the hills of Baluchistan in the north-west. In the Indus river valley, improved techniques permitted storage of wheat and barley beyond daily needs and cities grew up at Harappa and Mohenjodaro around 2300 B.C., creating a civilization more ad-vanced than that of the Aryans who came later.

The sewage system and work-ers' houses outside the citadel were of better construction than many of their modern equiva-lents. Among their domesticated animals was a major Indian con-tribution to the world's dinner tables—the chicken.

Modern archaeology suggests that this Indus Valley civilization was destroyed not, as subsequent chroniclers claimed, by Aryan conquerors, but by Indus river floods when it changed course, perhaps due to earthquake, about 1700 B.C.

The Hindus' Ancestors

The Aryans, as the Hindus label their forefathers, arrived on the scene 200 years later. Originally from southern Russia or central Asia, they migrated to Mesopota-mia and then northern Iran be-fore entering India through the Hindu Kush. Fair-skinned cattle-breeders to whom the cow was especially sacred, they took to agriculture in the Punjab, land of the "Five Rivers", after wars against the dark-skinned Dasas, who became their slaves.

Without archaeological evi-dence, the early years of the Indo-Aryans can be deduced only from the later writings of the *Rig-Veda* (priestly hymns), *Puranas* (an-cient tales of kings and gods) and the great epic poems of the *Maha-bharata* and *Ramayana*. These provided the basis for Hinduism, and the epics' heroic battles (see p.171) suggest there was a pro-longed struggle for land-rights over the fertile plains north and east of modern Delhi, followed by invasions of the south and wars against hunters in the Vindhya mountains.

If the ancient writings give only a very general and romanticized view of events, they offer a more precise picture of how Indo-Aryan society was organized, with many features that have lasted to the present day. The Aryans' prolonged wars against the indigenous peoples established the military leaders as kings with a hereditary divinity, which the *Brahmans* (priests) bestowed in exchange for the protection of a privileged position of their own. The kings have gone, but not the Brahmans.

The caste-system was already taking shape. Before the conquests, the Aryans were organized in three classes: warriors, priests and commoners. Then, to avoid assimilation with the dark-skinned Dasa slaves, they established four distinct categories known as *varna*, literally "colour".

As possessors of the magical powers associated with ritual sacrifice and especially the sacred utterance, the Brahmans were originally sole interpreters of the Vedic scriptures. Thus they laid down a religiously sanctioned social pecking-order with themselves in first place, followed by *Kshatriyas* (warriors), *Vaishyas* (cultivators and traders) and *Shudras* (serfs and those of mixed blood).

This hierarchic organization became more elaborate as the division of labour became more complicated. The increased number of occupational groups were subsequently defined as *jati* (sub-castes), often living in separate villages. The caste preserved its "purity" by avoiding intermarriage and the sharing of meals with other castes. Outside all caste were the lowliest of all, the Untouchables, originally mainly aboriginals.

By 600 B.C., the Indo-Aryans had formed several monarchies in the Ganga plain, surrounded by smaller tribes resisting the Brahmanic orthodoxy and the authoritarian rule that went with it.

Within the monarchies, independent-minded thinkers took to the asceticism that has characterized spiritual life in India ever since. The Brahmans cannily countered the threat to their authority by absorbing many of the new ideas into the orthodox teachings. But the tribes were less amenable and became the breeding-ground for two important new religions, both espousing doctrines of *ahimsa* (non-violence): Jainism, founded by a chief of the Jnatrikas near modern Patna, and Buddhism, by a prince of the Sakyas in the foothills of the Himalayas, in what is now Nepal.

While the Aryan kingdoms fought for control of the Ganga valley, new invaders were making their appearance at India's northwest frontiers. Cyrus, Emperor of Persia, crossed the Hindu Kush mountains into the Indus valley

21

around 530 B.C. While Brahman and Persian scholars exchanged ideas, Indian merchants copied the Persian coin system. Rock-inscriptions left by Emperor Darius probably inspired the pillar-edicts of Indian Emperor Ashoka in the 3rd century B.C.

Ajanta's cave-temples provided refuge from flood and plague for Buddhist and Jain monks.

The more spectacular invasion by Alexander the Great of Macedonia in 326 B.C. ended the Persian presence in India. But apart from opening up trade with Asia Minor and the eastern Mediterranean and designing the turreted howdah seat for riding the much admired elephants, the Greeks left no lasting impact on India itself during the two-year campaign.

Alexander's dreams of an

Indian empire extending eastwards across the Ganga plain were blocked by mutinous troops fed up with upset stomachs, the monsoon, the harsh terrain and the unexpectedly tough Indian military opposition. With battle-wounds that were to hasten his death three years later, he turned reluctantly westwards to Babylon, leaving just a couple of governors on the north-west frontier.

Ashoka's Empire

Meanwhile, in the Ganga valley power-struggle, Magadha (modern Bihar) emerged as the dominant kingdom, with Chandragupta Maurya (321–297 B.C.) as its ruler and founder of India's first imperial dynasty. His capital, Pataliputra (modern Patna), was probably the world's largest city at the time.

In the vacuum left by Alexander, Chandragupta extended his rule to the north-west with a campaign against the Greek forces of Seleucus Nikator. It ended in a profitable marriage alliance with the Greeks, made attractive to the latter by Indian gifts of elephants and aphrodisiacs. Then Chandragupta turned to more sober thoughts, converted to Jainism and starved to death at the temple of Sravanabelagola in southern India.

His son Bindusara also liked to combine imperial ambitions with a taste for good living and philosophy. He expanded the Maurya empire southwards to Mysore and raised eyebrows in the western world by asking King Antiochus for gifts of Greek wine, figs and a sophist. Antiochus was happy to send the wine and figs but would not consent to the brain-drain.

To control the land and sea routes to the south, the Mauryas needed still to conquer the eastern kingdom of Kalinga (modern Orissa). The task was left to Bindu-sara's heir Ashoka, admired by Indians as the greatest of their rulers, perhaps for his special knack of combining tough authoritarianism with a high moral sense of righteousness.

Ashoka began his reign (269–232 B.C.) in ruthless style, liquidating all his rivals for the throne before turning to the conquest of Kalinga in 260 B.C. By his own account, this left 100,000 dead on the battlefield, with many more dying, probably from subsequent famine and disease, while 150,000 were taken captive.

These details can be gathered from one of the famous inscriptions that Ashoka left as testimony to his reign on rocks and pillars throughout the country. The inscription on the conquest of Kalinga also shows how "he of gentle visage and beloved of the gods", as he describes himself, was filled with remorse and converted to the non-violent teachings of Buddha. But Buddhism's metaphysical implications seem to have interested him less than its moral example for his far-flung subjects to unite, under him, in a spirit of peace and fellowship.

To oversee the new spirit, Ashoka turned the old Brahmanic concept of *dharma* (righteousness) into an instrument of public policy, enforced by his Officers of Righteousness.

The imperial administration demanded a huge bureaucracy, with superintendents, accountants and clerks overseeing commerce, storehouses, forestry, armoury, weights and measures, goldsmiths, prostitutes, ships, cows, horses, elephants, chariots and infantry.

Southernmost India remained independent, but Ashoka had his hands full with an empire that now extended north to Kashmir and east to Bengal. In the 50 years following Ashoka's death, Mauryan power declined. Agriculture was not productive enough to provide for the empire's expansion and the unwieldy bureaucracy couldn't keep its loyalties straight with the too-rapid turnover in rulers vying for Ashoka's throne.

Invaders Galore

In the free-for-all that followed the break-up of the Mauryan empire, a succession of new foreign invaders appeared on the northwest frontier. The first to arrive were Bactrian Greeks left in the Afghan hills by Alexander's successors. They got as far as the Punjab, welcomed by Indian scholars for their new ideas on medicine, astronomy and astrology. The Greek innovation of casting horoscopes has remained an Indian passion ever since.

Joined nearby by Iranian kings known as Pahlavas (a dynasty claimed by the 20th-century

Shah), the Greeks were overrun in the 1st century B.C. by bands of Scythian nomads known to the Indians as Shakas. They in turn moved on to the Ganga valley when another wave of nomads, the Yueh-chi from Central Asia, swept across the frontier.

Emerging in A.D. 78 victorious from the struggles between the Yueh-chi and the Shakas, the great king Kanishka of the Kushan tribe established an empire over the northern half of India and into Central Asia. His reign was one of considerable prosperity, making India a trade centre between the western world and China.

Kanishka was a revered champion of Buddhism, promoting the Mahayana (Great Vehicle) school that for the first time attributed to Buddha a quasi-divinity. Benefiting from Kanishka's enthusiastic patronage of the arts, it led to the creation of the first bronze and stone sculptures of Buddha. Buddhist and Jain merchants prospered with the new east-west trade and were able to finance the magnificently sculpted cave-temples in the Deccan.

The arts also flourished in southern India during these early centuries of our modern era. Madurai was the lively cultural centre of Dravidian poets, actors, singers, musicians, and dancers who were precursors of the Hindu *devadasi* temple-prostitutes.

Gupta Glory

The Gupta dynasty, founded by Chandra Gupta I (an obscure Bihari landowner), rose to power in the early 4th century A.D. By marriage-alliance and conquest, the Guptas established an empire from Bengal across to the Punjab and from Kashmir down to the Deccan.

Samudra Gupta was the great warrior of the clan, launching lightning raids through the jungles of the peninsula to snatch the gold of the southern kingdoms. The Guptas added to their treasuries by capturing the western sea-ports and their trade with the Arabs. They turned their noses up at trade with the declining and falling Romans. China proved more profitable, offering silk, musk and amber to obtain India's spices, jewels and perfumes, as well as parakeets for the ladies' boudoirs and monkeys for their kitchen-pots.

The Gupta empire began to crumble in the middle of the 5th century with the onslaught of a new band of foreign invaders, the so-called White Huns. They were not clearly linked to the Huns of Attila but their ferocious extermination of Buddhists does suggest a certain affinity. The White Huns seized the Punjab, Kashmir and a large part of the western Ganga plain before being chased out again.

In the 7th century, one strong

25

king, Harsha Vadhana, reigned for some 40 years over most of northern India, encouraging both Buddhist monks and Brahman priests to participate in his philosophical discussions. Sages developed the strict physical and spiritual discipline of yoga and the profound metaphysical speculations of Vedanta.

In southern India, power was shared by the plundering Pallavas based in Kanchipuram and the Pandyas and Cholas vying for control of Thanjavur (Tanjore). With their *bhakti* movement, the Tamils brought a new devotional warmth to the hitherto rigid Brahmanic ritual of Hinduism. The rock-temples of Mahabalipuram were a high point in southern architecture and it was Pallavan artists from Kanchipuram who influenced and may even have helped to build the great temples at Angkor Wat in Cambodia and Borobudur in Java.

Islam Comes to India

Arab trade with India had long whetted the appetites of the Moslems, and when Indian pirates plundered their ships off the coast of Sind in 711, it provoked a full-fledged invasion. The governor of Chaldea (now Iraq) sent troops with 6,000 horses and 6,000 camels to conquer the Sind rajas and offer the infidels the alternative of conversion to Islam or death.

When closer inspection revealed that Hinduism, however idolatrous, was a serious religion with an unmanageable number of faithful to treat in this manner, another solution had to be found. The Hindus, along with a community of Parsis who had just fled to India from an earlier Moslem persecution in Persia, were given the privileged status of *dhimmi*, dues-paying non-believers.

For nearly 300 years, Islamic conquest in India was confined to this Arab trading community in Sind. At the end of the 10th century, tribesmen from Turkistan, driven to Afghanistan by westward Chinese expansion, set up their own state at Ghazni and began raids across the Indian border to plunder the great treasuries of Hindu temples.

Sweeping through the Punjab and Gujarat to the western end of the Ganga valley at Mathura and Kanauj, Mahmud of Ghazni (997–1030) used these murderous raids more to finance his empire in Persia and Turkistan than to establish any permanent foothold in India.

Mahmud smashed the infidels' idols and destroyed their temples as he went, but was nonetheless cultured enough to use the booty to build a library, museum and splendid mosque when he got

South Indian carving inspired artists throughout South-east Asia.

back home to Ghazni. If Moslems saw him as a righteous militant, and Hindus as a brutal monster, neither denied him his title of "Sword of Islam". To understand his ambiguous image, compare Europe's heroic Crusaders going on their holy rampage round about the same time.

There was no concerted Indian response to the Islamic invasions because the various kingdoms were preoccupied with wars of conquest among themselves. The Rajput warrior-clans fought each other for control in what is now Rajasthan, the Kathiawar peninsula and as far east as Khajuraho. The Turco-Afghan invaders were regarded as a transient phenomenon that would either disappear or, like others before them, be swallowed up by the great subcontinent.

A Sultan for Delhi

At the end of the 12th century the Turks came to stay. The Sultan Mohammed of Ghur and his Mameluke (slave) general Qutb-ud-din Aybak seized Ghazni in 1173 and invaded India with their Afghan forces. The Rajputs made a belated alliance and fought valiantly from one desert fortress to another, but their elephants could not match their opponents' fast Central Asian horses and Afghan cavalry firing their superior crossbows at the gallop. By 1193, the Turks were masters in Peshawar, Lahore and Delhi.

The sultan returned to Ghazni and left Qutb-ud-din in Delhi in charge of his Indian conquests. The conquerors moved east to take Bengal in 1202, destroying *en route* major centres of Buddhism such as the university of Nalanda.

When his master was assassinated in 1206, Qutb-ud-din proclaimed himself Sultan of Delhi, head of India's first Islamic dynasty. The sultanate lasted 320 years, but the new sultan ruled only four years before dying in a fall from his polo pony.

After the first oppressive shock, the Turks proved to be a shot in the arm for the sluggish state of affairs in India. The Persian language spoken at court enriched the literature and combined with the Sanskrit-based dialects of northern India to create the widely-spoken Hindustani. Painting and architecture were infused with new life, roads were paved and, by the 14th century, Delhi was pronounced by a north African Arab traveller, Ibn Batuta, to be the most magnificent city in the Moslem world.

Qutb-ud-Din celebrated his Delhi conquest with a tower to survey the city.

29

Conversion to Islam was encouraged as a means of social advancement rather than forced. Those Rajputs who didn't take advantage of this were able to sharpen their hereditary martial skills in constant guerrilla warfare.

For their part, the Turks adopted Indian cuisine and costume as more appropriate to the climate, together with a modified form of the Hindu caste-system. Highest were those of foreign extraction, Turks, Arabs, Afghans and Persians, known as *ashraf*, "honourable". Then came upper-caste converts from Hinduism, followed by the "clean" occupational castes of merchants and artisans, and lastly the "unclean" occupations of scavengers, etc.

Among the early rulers, it's worth noting the first—and last—Moslem woman to rule in India, Qutb-ud-din's granddaughter Raziyya. "Wise, just and generous," a contemporary Moslem historian said of her, "she was endowed with all the qualities befitting a king, but she was not born of the right sex and so, in the estimation of men, all the virtues were worthless." Three years of her wisdom, justice and generosity were all they could take before they murdered her.

What they seemed to want was tough despots like Ala-ud-din Khalji (1296–1316), who drove Mongol invaders back across the Afghan frontier in 1306 and then moved the next year down through the peninsula to its southernmost tip.

Ala-ud-din's successors did little to assert control of the briefly conquered territory. The south remained under the domination of the Hindu kingdom of Vijayanagar for the next 250 years.

The Delhi sultanate under the Tughlaq dynasty could no longer hold its own in the north, and breakaway Moslem kingdoms began to form in Bengal and the Deccan.

The end was hastened by someone who made the earlier Moslem invaders seem like pussy cats: the Mongol Timur the Lame, the "barbarous and bloody Tamburlaine" of Elizabethan playwright Christopher Marlowe. On the grounds that the sultans were bad Moslems, too soft on their subjects, he cut through Delhi in 1398, slaughtering thousands of Hindus and carrying off thousands more as slaves. He left behind him famine and pestilence, with the Turks' Indian empire in splinters, passing into the hands of Afghan horse-breeders, the Lodi, who were in turn to succumb to Timur's descendants, the Mughals.

Down on the Malabar coast, the great Portuguese explorer Vasco da Gama dropped anchor in 1498, paving the way for his countrymen's settlement at Goa. The merchants wanted to get the spice-trade away from the Arabs, fearing that the enrichment of the North African Maghreb was a threat to Christian Europe.

With them came Catholic missionaries who found their best customers among low-caste Hindus. St. Francis Xavier, who was there in 1548, began his mission among the pearl fishermen of Goa, before sailing on to Japan. To deal with small communities of Jews and Nestorian Christian "heretics", who had settled on the Malabar coast in the mists of antiquity, the Archbishop of Goa opened a local branch of the Holy Inquisition.

The merchants at first tried the soft sell, offering cloth, wine and necklaces for ivory and gold, but the seasoned Indian traders of Calicut were insulted at being taken for the kind of "natives" who could be bought with cheap hooch and glass baubles. So the Portuguese turned to the harder sell of their naval batteries, driving off an Egyptian trading fleet in 1509 to control the Malabar coast. With practically no women in their colony, Portuguese soldiers took wives among the Indians. Many Goans of today are descended from them or from converts who took the surname of their Portuguese sponsors at baptism.

The Great Mughals

The new conquerors of northern India did not come uninvited. The Afghan governors of the Sind and the Punjab, hoping for more autonomy than they had under the high-handed Sultan Ibrahim Lodi in Delhi, called on Babur, the Tiger, King of Kabul.

Babur, descendant not only of terrible Timur the Lame but also, on his mother's side, of Genghis Khan, accepted the governors' welcome as liberator but made no promises. With cannons, hitherto unknown in India, his 8,000 men crushed the Sultan Ibrahim's 50,000 at the battle of Panipat, north of Delhi.

It was the morning of April 21, 1526, beginning of the new Indian empire of the Mughals*. Babur quickly captured Delhi and Agra, with the fiercest resistance coming once more from the Rajputs, before he could move east and complete the conquest after victory over the Afghan chiefs of Bihar and Bengal in 1529. He died a year later.

His heir Humayun preferred opium and astrology to the affairs of state and was driven out of India across into Persia in 1540 by Babur's general, Sher Shah, who proved a much more able ruler. In

*Mughal, or Mogul, is the same word, etymologically, as Mongol, but the latter refers to all the followers of Genghis Khan while Mughal is reserved for Babur's descendants and followers.

31

just five years, the general built new roads, created a royal postal service and set the pattern of Mughal administration for the next two centuries before dying in battle and leaving the throne to inept successors and the return of Humayun.

Straightened out for a while, Humayun came back in 1555 with a Persian army to recapture the Punjab, Delhi and Agra. But the next year, the opium habit caused his death in a silly accident (see p. 67). The one clever thing he did was leave a son named Akbar.

Now Jalal-ud-din Mohammed Akbar (1556–1605) was a real emperor. Typical of his genius was the eclectic new religion he offered his subjects: the Divine Faith *(Din-Ilahi)* intended to satisfy both orthodox Moslems and those like himself and his Hindu subjects who appreciated the idea of a semi-divine ruler.

Keen to win the allegiance of the Hindus (he certainly seems to be the favourite Moslem ruler of Hindu historians), Akbar abolished most of the discriminatory taxes on non-Moslems. He recruited Rajputs for his army after marrying a daughter of Raja Bharmal of Amber, but did not flinch at massacring another, less friendly, Rajput's 8,000 soldiers at Chittorgarh.

Despite repeated efforts, Akbar could not extend his empire south. In 1565, the Moslem sultanates of the Deccan had together overthrown the great Hindu empire of Vijayanagar with massive pillage and slaughter, but they weren't about to hand it all to Akbar.

Though illiterate, Akbar had enormous intellectual curiosity. He preferred Sufi mysticism to orthodox Islam, but was eclectic in his religious tastes, debating with Brahmans, Jain monks, Parsi Zoroastrians, Sikhs and Jesuits. Orthodox Moslems began to worry that Islam was being abandoned and sporadic rebellions sprang up in Bengal, Bihar and the Punjab.

While Akbar was off fighting in the Deccan in 1601, his son claimed the throne. The emperor rushed back to reassert his power but died soon after, poisoned, it's said, by his own son. The new emperor called himself Jahangir, "World Seizer". But once on the throne, Jahangir (1605–1627) lost his interest in seizing the world and left affairs of state to his wife Nur Jahan.

Jahangir was more interested in writing poetry, drinking a great deal of wine and taking summer excursions up to Kashmir. In his capital at Agra, Persian culture dictated tastes in dress, décor, manners and morals, subtly en-

Humayun's tomb: religion was not his opium, opium was his religion.

riched by the Hindu culture of the Rajputs in literature, cuisine and sexuality.

If the peasants were squeezed by taxes to pay for the luxury of Mughal court life, it was a boon for the country's artisans—goldsmiths, jewellers and weavers. In the generally dissolute atmosphere, highway banditry increased and district governors shared the booty in exchange for a pardon when the bandits were captured.

Jahangir shared his father's religious tolerance, being equally at home with Hindu ascetics and Jesuit missionaries. He was so polite to the latter that they reported to Rome he was ripe for conversion. In fact, he was just being polite.

His son Shahjahan was the biggest spender of all the Mughals. He lavished millions on jewel-encrusted palaces and mosques, blowing at least one million pounds sterling (in the currency of the day) on the gold, diamonds, emeralds, rubies and sapphires for his Peacock Throne. But the imperial treasury allotted only 5,000 rupees per week for the plague and famine victims of 1631.

Of several hundred women in the emperor's harem, his only love was the now legendary Mumtaz-Mahal ("Exalted of the Palace"), by whom he had 14 children. She died in childbirth, in the year of the pestilence, and Shahjahan built the most famous memorial a man ever offered to the woman he loved: the mausoleum of the Taj Mahal.

With the Mughals' customary filial loyalty, Shahjahan's son Aurangzeb (1658–1707), overthrew his father and imprisoned him in the Agra fort for the last eight years of his life. The days of luxury and artistic glory were over. A pious Moslem, puritanical in clothes and personal tastes, Aurangzeb banished music from the court and burned portraits of princes as breaches of the Islamic taboo on graven images.

Gone, too, was religious tolerance. Sikhs were slaughtered, Hindu temples in Varanasi and Mathura were destroyed, the building of new temples forbidden. The old taxes on non-Moslems were brought back and Hindu merchants were forced to pay for their goods double the duty imposed on Moslems.

Aurangzeb concentrated on streamlining the lax administration left by his predecessors. But he almost bankrupted the realm with his campaigns to expand the empire to the south and battles against Hindu rebels in Rajputana and the northern plains.

The most significant resistance he had to face was that of the Marathas, in what is today the western state of Maharashtra, around Bombay. They were led by Sivaji (1627–1680), ruthless bandit, courageous military leader, authentic Hindu folk-hero. Starting out from Pune (Poona), Sivaji's Marathas fought the Deccan sultans at Bijapur, the Mughals at Purandar. Aurangzeb forced him finally to submit, but his humiliating reception at court sent him back out on the war-path. Sivaji had himself crowned king of the Marathas and, to pay his soldiers, plundered the country all the way east to Madras.

The British Arrive

Meanwhile, by the middle of the 17th century, Dutch and British armed merchant-ships had successfully broken the Portuguese blockade to set up their East India Companies on both coasts.

Arriving in 1608, the British took only five years to get their foot in the Indian door, at the western port of Surat, north of Bombay. The Company won trading rights by destroying the Portuguese fleet and taking over the protection of the Moslem pilgrimage ships to Mecca. No hard feelings; the Portuguese made a present of Bombay to King Charles II in 1661 as part of the dowry of Catherine of Braganza. The Indians were not consulted.

The Company built its east coast installations in 1642 just down the road from the Dutch, at the Tamil village of Mandaraz, pronounced by the British "Madras". Further north, on the Hooghly river in the Ganga delta, the British gradually gained the upper hand over its European rivals, now including the French, for the lucrative Bengali trade that was to create, by 1698, Calcutta.

The Mughal empire was disintegrating. It had five rulers in the 12 years after the death of Aurangzeb. Bengal, Bihar and Rajputana were going their separate ways. The Sikhs reacted violently to persecution, and the Marathas spread their power from Gujarat to Orissa. In 1739, Nadir Shah of Persia invaded India and sacked Delhi in time-honoured murderous manner, carrying off the Peacock Throne (broken up after his assassination a few years later).

Things were hotting up among the Europeans, too, as the British under Robert Clive, brilliant Company-clerk-turned-soldier, won a long hard-fought campaign against the French for control of the Coromandel coast around Madras.

Fearing the Europeans would start carving up Bengal as they had the region around Madras, the Nawab (Moslem prince) Siraj-ud-daula launched a surprise attack on the British settlement in Calcutta on the blindingly hot day of June 20, 1756. Those who did not flee to the ships were thrown into Fort William's tiny prison-cell, already known even before this infamous day as the Black Hole (it was the local term for the lock-up).

It's still being debated whether 123 suffocated and 23 survived or "only" 43 died with 21 survivors, but at the time the horror was motivation enough for Clive to crush Siraj-ud-daula one year later at the Battle of Plassey. Clive became governor and placed his own nawab on the throne, in exchange for a gift from the lucky man of £500,000, shared between Clive and the Company. On behalf of the Company, he annexed 2,330 square kilometres (900 sq. mi.) of land south of Calcutta to provide rents for the upkeep of the British settlement and to guarantee himself a lifetime income of £30,000 a year. The rise to British Empire in India had begun.

Installing the Raj

The influx of Indian merchants, including many Jains, Parsis and Jews, quickly turned Bombay, Madras and Calcutta into big cities and the Company discovered a knack for large-scale administration. A high sense of public service and integrity was gradually supplementing, if not totally replacing, what Clive himself called the "fighting, chicanery, intrigues, politics and Lord knows what".

In return for fixed payments to the emperor and local rulers, Company officials took over the job of revenue-collection. By creating a well-paid civil service, Clive's successors, Warren Hastings and Lord Cornwallis, stemmed the practice whereby collectors padded their salaries with kickbacks from the rulers or private deals as individual entrepreneurs. With the new title of Governor-General, Hastings and then Cornwallis were now directly responsible to the British government rather than the East India Company. Britain was taking India more seriously.

But the new high-mindedness had in it the seeds of future discontent. Indians were removed from key positions in the administration because Cornwallis considered them not yet up to the stricter ethical standards being introduced. It took a long time for them to be readmitted to positions of responsibility.

Clive's example in Calcutta set the pattern for extending territorial control around the country. In the south, Tipu Sultan of Mysore was a serious menace to Madras until Governor-General Arthur Wellesley, future Duke of Wellington, personally masterminded his defeat. Madras sovereignty duly extended inland.

Wellesley then turned on the Marathas, whose various clans controlled the puppet Mughal emperor in Delhi and much of central India. A couple of brilliant victories gained for Britain control of Orissa and other territories, but London decided all that bellicose energy would be better directed against Napoleon and called him home.

When territory wasn't acquired by conquest—Sind from Baluchi princes, Punjab and Kashmir from the Sikhs, Maharashtra and Delhi from the Marathas or Assam from Burma—the British quite simply annexed it by socalled Principles of Lapse and Paramountcy. If a ruler died without direct heir, his state "lapsed" into the hands of the British. If a state, after repeated warnings, was judged guilty of misgovernment, it was annexed by the Paramount Power, i.e. the British.

Schools and colleges were established. Calcutta became the centre of a vigorous free press and the intellectual capital of India.

In 1834, regional rupees of differing value were minted, with the face of the Mughal emperor, by then living on a British pension. The next year, a national rupee of unitary value was issued, with the face of the King of England. For the efficient running of the empire, the British installed railways, better roads, the telegraph and stamp-post. The Indians saw the other side of the Industrial Revolution as their raw cotton left for Manchester to come back as cloth much cheaper than their own weavers could ever manage.

Men of good will like Governor-General William Bentinck worked with missionaries and Indian reformers such as Brahman Ram Mohan Roy to legislate, in 1829, against the practice of widows becoming *sati* by throwing themselves on their husband's funeral pyre. Other campaigns were launched against female infanticide, slavery and murderous bands of Thugs (devotees of Kali) and dacoits (bandits) left to range the countryside when the Maratha armies were disbanded.

Although Indians in regular contact with the British gradually assimilated their language and behaviour—nobody more so than the anglophile Parsis of Bombay—for the great majority, the British were offensively aloof. The Indians had known other conquerors, but however cruel or corrupt they might at times have been, at least they could get a sense of them as human beings. The British Raj, entrenched in clubs and cantonments, remained resolutely separate.

Mutiny and Reform

The immediate cause of the Indian Mutiny of 1857 was symptomatic of British insensitivity to the people they ruled. Indian troops had been trained to bite the cartridges before loading their rifles. But some of the cartridges had been greased with animal fat and the Indians felt they were being forced to ingest either fat from the cow, sacrilegious to the Hindus, or lard from the pig, abomination to the Moslems. Having too often suffered slights of incomprehension or contempt for their religious customs in the past, they refused to believe it was not a deliberate trick. Mutiny broke out at the garrison of Meerut, 40 kilometres (25 mi.) north of Delhi.

The cartridge blunder became a pretext for avenging other grievances, with troops rallying around the puppet emperor and rulers dispossessed by the Principles of Lapse or Paramountcy. Confined to north and central India, the mutineers invaded Delhi, Kanpur (Cawnpore) and Lucknow, looting treasuries, breaking open jails and slaughtering British men, women and chil-

dren. The British retaliated with equal savagery, both against the mutineers and against civilians in the country through which relief columns passed. The Emperor Bahadur Shah, last of the proud Mughals, was exiled to Burma.

Nothing could more aptly epitomize the Mutiny's good and bad results, from an Indian point of view, than the name of the legislation that followed: the 1858 Act for Better Government of India. The British evidently saw the need to improve life for the Indians but also decided to tighten their imperial hold.

The East India Company was replaced by a Government of India with a Viceroy answering to a Secretary of State for India in London. The bureaucracy was to be streamlined, the army reorganized to raise the ratio of British to Indians.

At the same time, Indian education was greatly expanded, though less successfully in rural areas where it was considered better to be a good peasant than a bad clerk. Queen Victoria, who in 1876 would add the title Empress of India, proclaimed that the Indian Civil Service would be open to "our subjects of whatever race and creed". Not a lot of Indians could afford the trip to Britain to take the examination.

But Indian lawyers were at a premium—Indians love litigation and it proved ideal training for the country's future politicians. Politics in India had always been clandestine, because it was so often fatal to express an opinion on the wrong, i.e. losing, side. Now open political debate flourished,

East really does meet West in the Mughal Gothic of Bombay's Victoria Terminus.

especially in Calcutta where Karl Marx was much appreciated.

Indian entrepreneurs were beginning to come into their own with cotton mills opening up in Bombay, Ahmedabad, Kanpur and Madras, but the new tea gardens of Assam and Darjeeling were a strictly British affair. Indian agricultural products found new markets in Europe with the opening of the Suez Canal in 1869.

In the arts, native talent had succumbed to European tastes. Architecture was more often the work of engineers than architects and monumental sculpture inevitably ordered from Victorian Britain rather than from local artists. The bright spot was the creation in 1871 of the Archaeological Survey to preserve ancient monuments in a land where the reciprocal vandalism of Hindus and Moslems had been more of a tradition than restoration. British soldiers hunting tiger in the jungle were uncovering temples and palaces the Indians no longer knew existed.

Fighting for Self-Rule

The Indian National Congress, the country's first political party, held its inaugural meeting in Bombay in 1885. Largely a group of liberal Hindu and Parsi intellectuals, lawyers, teachers and journalists supported by a few progressive British (its first president was an Englishman), it was more national in purpose than in representativeness. It had no connection with the peasants and was distrusted by conservative landlords and by all but a few Moslems. The goal of *swaraj* ("self-rule"), proclaimed in 1906, was interpreted by a moderate Left Centre group as responsible government within the British Empire and by a breakaway revolutionary Extreme Left group as complete independence.

There were both progressive and reactionary sides to the new national consciousness. After years of subservience to the West, artists returned to Indian themes in their literature, theatre and music. Indians applauded the decision of Lord Ripon to allow Indian magistrates to try British defendants in criminal cases. But attempts at social reform such as protecting child-brides against rape by their husbands were fought by traditionalist Hindus in Calcutta and Pune with cries of "religion in danger".

Self-assertion was the order of the day. After years of relative tranquillity, communal hostilities broke out between Hindus and Moslems. In Maharashtra, a cult grew up around the flamboyant Maratha leader Sivaji (see p. 34–35) as a symbol of Hindu nationalism directed not only against the British but also the Moslems whom Sivaji had fought all his life. Hindu fundamentalists took to the streets to protest Moslem cow-killings. There was a movement to convert Indian Moslems and Christians back to the "national" religion. For their part, the Moslems sought to purify Islamic practice of the Hindu rituals which had accrued over the years.

The caste-system, too, was affected by the new spirit. Untouchables pressed for better treatment, but their cause was not helped by the activism of American missionaries and the Salvation Army who gave other castes a good excuse to resist "foreign interference".

The dynamic Lord Curzon, viceroy from 1899 to 1905, was driven by a lofty imperial vision of the British role in India. His grandiose style of life in the Viceregal Residence in Calcutta or summer palace in the hill station of Simla was worthy of the Mughal emperors in their heyday.

Highly active in the excavation and restoration of temples and palaces, Curzon also did more than any of his predecessors to cut through bureaucratic red tape, adding some 9,000 kilometres (5,500 mi.) of new railway lines, working to modernize farming with an agricultural research institute, and making the irrigation works a model for Asia and Africa. But Indians resented his arrogant refusal to consult them, rioting over an ill-considered partition of Bengal.

In 1911, King George V became the first British monarch to visit India. He celebrated the fact by announcing that the imperial capital would be moved from Calcutta to a new city to be built in Delhi. (The Bengalis' chagrin at this was only slightly soothed by reversal of the Curzon partition.) Royal architects Edwin Lutyens and Herbert Baker laid out a sprawling, monumental New Delhi with triumphal arch, viceregal palace, gigantic government buildings and sweeping avenues radiating from circles (for easy riot control), the stuff of an empire meant to last forever.

Without giving up demands for self-determination, India fought enthusiastically at Britain's side in World War I, causing more than one Prussian general to blink at Rajput and Sikh princes leading Indian infantrymen through the trenches of France.

In 1917, self-determination seemed nearer when London announced its plan for "the progressive realization of responsible government in India as an integral part of the (British) Empire." The British were not letting go, but a new Government of India Act two years later promised Indians real executive power at the head of provincial ministries for education, public works, health and agriculture. Moderate

Indians were delighted, revolutionaries saw it as a foot in the door, while many shocked British officials retired rather than serve under Indian ministers.

But there was trouble in the streets. The riots over Bengal's partition had led to new laws allowing political trials without jury and internment without trial. Popular protest in the big cities in 1919 at first took the non-violent form of a *hartal*, a time-honoured Indian "strike" called when the soul was shocked by an injustice. It was the characteristic idea of a new leader, Mohandas Karamchand Gandhi, dubbed Mahatma, "Great Soul", by poet Rabindranath Tagore.

Son of a Gujarati merchant, Gandhi returned to India in 1915 after working as a lawyer defending the rights of the Indian community in South Africa. The moral strength of Gandhi's non-violent philosophy was immediately tested in the Punjab, where the *hartal* erupted into riots. In Amritsar, the troops of General Reginald Dyer fired without warning on a prohibited mass meeting, leaving 379 dead and over 1,200 wounded. Gradualist reform was discredited and civil unrest became a permanent feature of everyday life.

Declaring "cooperation in any shape or form with this satanic government is sinful", Gandhi advocated boycott of elections and withdrawal from government office. Moderates held on to their hard-won office, but the election boycott was at least 33 per cent successful.

Abandoning European dress for his now legendary white cotton *dhoti* (loin-cloth) and shawl and drawing spiritual guidance from all the great religions of India, the Mahatma had become the simple but powerful symbol of the nation. He championed the cause of the Untouchables and defended the rights of village artisans and peasants, but his non-violent movement could not stop the escalating riots among the religious communities.

Worried by the spread of his civil disobedience movement, the British jailed Gandhi in 1922 for two years. In jail at the same time, for "incitement to rebellion", was Congress Party militant Jawaharlal Nehru, British-educated but a Brahman intellectual as his honorary title of Pandit suggested and the Mahatma's favourite to lead India to independence.

Independence with Partition

British negotiators began to see independence as inevitable, but few seemed to understand the vital role of the religious groups. Britain was blithely preparing a parliamentary democracy with majority rule, on the British model. But the overwhelming majority were Hindus, and Hindus,

42

Moslems and Sikhs had been killing each other for centuries.

Nehru's Congress Party, largely Hindu with a socialist leadership, wanted a parliamentary democracy. To provide a counterweight, British legislation reserved groups of parliamentary seats for religious minorities. But regions such as the Punjab and Bengal had such a complicated mixture of Hindus, Moslems and Sikhs that it was impossible to avoid fights over how separate constituencies were to be formed. The seeds of future trouble were sown.

The reserved-seat legislation gave the Moslems the basis for an

Gandhi led a march to the sea to protest the British salt tax.

alternative to an India in which they were only a quarter of the population: Partition. In 1930, the poet Muhammad Iqbal proposed a separate Moslem homeland in the north-west of India. A small group of Indian Moslems at Cambridge came up with the name Pakistan, taking the initials of Punjab, Afghania (N.W. Frontier Province), Kashmir and Sind (at the same time producing the word *pak*, meaning "pure") and adding "stan", the Persian suffix for "country". The Moslem League's campaign for Partition was led by the uncompromising London-trained Bombay lawyer, Muhammad Ali Jinnah.

Meanwhile, Gandhi, vehemently opposed to any dismemberment of the Indian nation, tried to weld the people together with fasts to uphold a spirit of love and, more politically, by focussing on the common adversary, the British, with stepped-up civil disobedience. His famous Salt March to the sea, to scoop up free salt and circumvent the hated British salt tax, landed more than 60,000 in jail.

Against this background of impatient militancy, World War II did not elicit the same Indian solidarity as the first. Indians once again courageously fought alongside the British, in Burma, the Middle East and Europe, but Gandhi called the British presence in India a provocation for Japanese invasion and was jailed yet again, for launching his "Quit India" campaign in 1942. Anti-British extremists even saw in the Japanese an Asian liberator.

Winston Churchill didn't want any kind of Indian independence, partitioned or otherwise, and so it was probably as well for India that he was defeated by Clement Attlee's Labour Party in 1945. With riots growing ever more bloody in Bengal, Bihar and the Punjab, the last viceroy, Lord Mountbatten, had a mandate to make Britain's departure from India as quick and smooth as possible. Quick it was, six months from his arrival in New Delhi, but not smooth.

Midnight on August 14–15, 1947, was a moment, in the words of Prime Minister Nehru, "when we step out from the old to the new, when an age ends, and when the soul of a nation, long suppressed, finds utterance."

Nehru got his Independence and Jinnah his Partition—a Pakistan in which its eastern Bengali portion was to break away 24 years later to become Bangladesh.

Bloodshed began as soon as Partition boundaries were announced. In east (Indian) Punjab, Hindus and Sikhs massacred Moslems, in west (Pakistani) Punjab, Moslems massacred Sikhs and Hindus. The massacres were followed by an exodus of millions from one country to the other and the convoys often ended in slaughter. Delhi itself was torn apart by communal rampages. The overall death toll was at least 500,000.

Gandhi rushed from Calcutta to Delhi to defend Moslems against further slaughter. In January 1948, he fasted for peace in the capital and to force the Indian government to pay Pakistan the amounts due in the Partition's division of assets. A Hindu fanatic, enraged by Gandhi's impartial defence of Moslem interests, shot him dead at a prayer meeting on January 30.

India Today

Elegant, sensitive and sophisticated, Pandit Nehru was probably also the strongest ruler India had known since the great Mughals and, like them, he founded a powerful dynasty. Rejecting his mentor Gandhi's faith in a village-based democracy, Nehru worked to make India a fully industrialized society on a basis of democratic socialism. Established industries had their taxes raised but were not nationalized. Foreign companies had to accept Indian financial participation and management.

He appropriated for the state much of the fabulous personal fortunes of the princes, but found it harder to curtail the power of entrenched land-owners who had extensive contacts with the more conservative elements inside his Congress Party.

Kashmir remained an unresolved problem of Partition. The Moslem majority in the Vale of Kashmir and Gilgit made it logically part of Pakistan, but most of the eastern region around Jammu was Hindu, as was the maharaja himself. Pathan tribesmen, with Pakistani backing, invaded Kashmir in 1947 in an attempt to force the issue, but were repulsed by Indian troops flown in when the maharaja hastily acceded to India. After brief but bitter fighting, Kashmir was divided between India and Pakistan along a cease-fire line, pending a plebiscite (which has never been held). An abortive Pakistani invasion in 1965 has left the question still distinctly moot.

Applying a principle of India's geographical integrity, Nehru regained French Pondicherry by negotiation after Independence and Portuguese Goa by force in 1961. He was less successful in his fight with China over territory on the frontier with Tibet.

Egalitarian and agnostic, Nehru passed laws against the injustices of the caste-system, child marriage and the general treatment of women in Hindu households, but centuries-old customs die hard. Before his death in 1964, he asked that his ashes be scattered in the Yamuna river at Delhi and the Ganga at

Allahabad, but without religious ritual. The mourning crowds ignored his wishes, uttered up prayers and cried: "Panditji has become immortal."

Coming to power in January 1966 (after the brief ministry of Lal Bahadur Shastri), Indira Gandhi soon proved strong enough in her own right for people to stop describing her as Nehru's daughter or "not related to Mahatma Gandhi". In fact, she learned much from both, the knack for power-politics of the one and the massive popular appeal of the other. She accelerated India's industrialization, particularly nuclear power, including a first atomic explosion in the Rajasthan desert in 1974. But her proudest achievement was the Green Revolution which modernized wheat and rice farming to give India for the first time

self-sufficiency in food production. Entrenched conservatism hampered her birth-control programmes to check the rocketing population growth.

Her tendency to tough authoritarianism was highlighted during the repressive state of national emergency she declared in 1975 (describing it as "disciplined democracy"), when she ordered mass arrests of opposition leaders who had charged her and her party with malpractice and corruption.

The electorate punished her in 1977 with three years in the wilderness, then brought her back with a huge majority. But her second term was beset with the problems of regional unrest, most notably in Assam in the northeast, where local massacres left 3,000 dead, and in the Punjab where Sikh militants staged violent demonstrations for greater autonomy and even independence. It was her order to the Indian Army in 1984 to attack armed militants inside the Sikhs' most sacred Golden Temple in Amritsar, resulting in 800 dead, that led to her assassination in Delhi five months later by two Sikh members of her security guard. Hindus rampaged through Sikh communities and the round of communal violence resumed.

Those who followed her, including her son, Rajiv Gandhi, were beset with problems of corruption and communal conflict. Meanwhile, India continued to modernize its industry, to face the challenges of an ever-growing population that threatens to outnumber even that of China by the beginning of the next century.

Modern India looms behind the age-old trade of Bombay fishermen.

HISTORICAL LANDMARKS

Prehistory c. 30,000–1500 B.C.		Stone Age peoples settle in India. First farmers in Baluchistan.
First Civilization 2300–1700 B.C.		Indus River valley civilization.
Indo-Aryan Migration 1500–530 B.C.	1500 530	Indo-Aryans enter India. Buddhism founded.
Persians and Greeks 530–326 B.C.	530 326	Persians invade Indus valley. Alexander crosses Indus into Punjab.
Mauryan Empire 321–185 B.C.	321 269–232	Chandragupta Maurya founds first Indian empire. Reign of Emperor Ashoka.
Nomad Invasions 185 B.C.–300 A.D.	100 B.C. 98 A.D.	Scythians and Yueh-chi invade. Kushan empire.
Gupta Empire 320–495 A.D.	320	Chandra Gupta founds empire enriched by trade with China.
Islam in India 711–1193	711 1001–1030	Arabs invade Sind. Mahmud of Ghazni plunders Punjab, Gujarat and Ganga valley.
Turco-Afghan Domination 1193–1526	1193 1336 1398	Turco-Afghan forces conquer Delhi, install sultanate. Foundation of Hindu kingdom of Vijayanagar in south. Timur the Lame (Tamberlaine) sacks Delhi.
Mughal Empire 1526–1756	1526 1556–1605 1605 1612 1642	Mughal empire begins. Reign of Emperor Akbar. Jahangir seizes Mughal throne. English merchants start trade in Surat (near modern Bombay). English establish East India Company in Madras.

	1646–1680	Sivaji leads Hindu Marathas against Mughals.
	1698	East India Company establishes settlement at Calcutta.
Rise of British Empire 1756–1858	1757	Battle of Plassey secures English hold on Bengal.
	1799	Defeat of Tipu Sultan.
	1803	British take Delhi.
	1849	Sikhs defeated, cede Punjab.
	1857	Indian Mutiny.
	1858	Last Mughal emperor exiled to Burma.
Road to Independence 1858–1947	1858	Better Government of India Act.
	1885	Indian National Congress founded.
	1911	George V first British monarch to visit India. Capital transferred from Calcutta to New Delhi.
	1919	British troops kill 379 at Amritsar.
	1930	Gandhi's Salt March.
	1947	Independence for India and Pakistan.
India Today 1947–	1947–64	Jawaharlal Nehru prime minister.
	1948	Mahatma Gandhi assassinated.
	1962	War with China.
	1965	Pakistani invasion of Kashmir repelled.
	1966–77	Indira Gandhi's first term.
	1974	Experimental atomic explosion in Rajasthan desert.
	1984	Indian Army storms Sikhs' Golden Temple. Indira Gandhi assassinated.
	1990	Communal violence in Kashmir.

RELIGIONS OF INDIA

Although the constitution of modern India describes it as a secular state, religion still plays a vital part in everyday life in its streets as well as in the architecture, sculpture and painting of its great monuments. A little background information to the major faiths may be helpful.

Hinduism

If it is more or less India's national cult, it's because Hinduism has something for everyone: mysticism and metaphysics for the scholars, colourful ceremony for ordinary people, austerity and sensuality, gentle tranquillity and violent frenzy.

Building on the ancient indigenous cults and the Vedic teachings of the Indo-Aryans, Hinduism began to take its present form around the end of the 4th century A.D. under popular pressure, particularly in the Dravidian south, for a more "accessible" religion. Devotional worship, with its more obvious appeal to the common people, replaced the esoteric sacrifices practised exclusively by the aristocratic Brahmans.

It is said there are 330 million gods in the complete Hindu pantheon, but they might equally be regarded as 330 million facets of one divinity, the three most important being Brahma, Vishnu and Shiva. These are often presented to Westerners as a trinity, though it is not really comparable to the Christian concept.

The "big three" are by no means accorded equal status. Vishnu, the preserver, is regarded by his worshippers as a benevolent universal god from whose navel a lotus grew, bearing Brahma, whose only task it was to create the world. Vishnu, usually represented as a four-armed god holding a mace, conch-shell, discus and lotus, has many incarnations, including fish, tortoise, boar, dwarf and, most famous of all, Krishna, who in turn appears as conquering hero, prolific flute-playing lover or mischievous little baby. Vishnu's wife Lakshmi is goddess of good fortune.

Shiva is the dancing destroyer-god, wearing a garland of skulls with snakes around his neck and arms. He is the god of time, the god of ascetics, the great sage deciding the fate of the world up in the Himalayas, with the waters of the Ganga flowing through his hair. Lord of beasts, king of dance, symbolized by the phallic lingam, Shiva is as passionate as Vishnu is serene. Just in case you think you have got it all clear,

No penetrating the inner world of a Hindu yogi.

remember that Vishnu also destroys by not preserving and Shiva preserves through the renewal arising from destruction.

Shiva's wife is the virtuous Parvati, who also appears in the form of the formidable Durga or Kali, goddess of terror.

By the 19th century, reformers such as the Bengali Brahman Ram Mohan Roy worked to rid Hinduism of its idolatry and other primitive practices. The self-immolation of widows, an act commonly known as *sati**, has practically disappeared, but the idols of monkey-god Hanuman and elephant-headed Ganesh, on taxi dashboards as well as at roadside temples, are still going strong. And nobody's about to deny the sanctity of the cow and her five products—milk, curd, butter, urine and dung.

Hindu ethics proclaim as the path to *moksha*, salvation, three principles in life: righteousness, prosperity honestly achieved and, not least, pleasure.

Central to the Hindu's confrontation with the often harsh realities of daily life is the concept of *karma*. Literally "work" or "deed", it implies the sum total of a person's acts in a previous existence which determines his present station in life. For the pre-

sent, it holds out the promise of a better reincarnation.

While this teaching has undoubtedly served to sustain the rigid hierarchy of the caste-system (see p. 21–22), it is not so "fatalistic" as some would have it. The Hindus say we cannot escape our *karma* but with good judgment and foresight, we can use it to our advantage.

Islam

It is, of course, not an Indian religion and that, in India, has been its problem. After a contact almost as old as Islam itself (the first Moslems, from Arabia, settled in India just 80 years after Mohammed's death), peaceful coexistence with Hinduism still seems difficult to achieve.

It's hard to imagine anything more different from Hinduism than a religion so hostile to all idolatry, fiercely attached to uncompromising monotheism, and with fundamentally egalitarian principles opposed, at least initially, to the caste-system. When *sufi* mystics or the great emperor Akbar attempted to achieve a synthesis between the two faiths, the orthodox on both sides resisted.

Hindu conversions to Islam, when not forced, were more often performed out of hope of social advancement under Moslem government than out of religious conviction. Nonetheless, Moslems

---

*A widow did not "commit" *sati*, she "became" *sati* (meaning "virtuous woman"), by throwing herself on her husband's funeral pyre.

Amritsar's Golden Temple is shrine and fortress to beleaguered Sikhs.

living in India today are mostly descendants of those converts and as fervent as their brethren in Pakistan or the Middle East.

They have the same divisions into Sunnites (adherents of the Sunna law expounded in Mohammed's own words and acts) and Shiites (followers of interpretations proposed by Mohammed's cousin Ali and his successors). Each day, the devout face Mecca, bow their foreheads to the ground and proclaim: "There is no god but God; and Mohammed is His Prophet."

Sikhism

The one attempt to create a strong, if embattled religion out of Hinduism and Islam is the faith of the Sikhs ("disciples").

Nanak, their founding *guru* (teacher), was born a Hindu in the Punjab in 1469 and reared on the egalitarian principles of Islam. He was strongly opposed to idolatry and the caste-system (which, as for Indian Moslems, subsequently proved too strong to resist). From Islam he took the idea of one God, but refused any such specific conception as Allah. He preferred to see God's manifestation, not unlike Hinduism, everywhere in the world He created.

Nanak's own teachings were

53

inscribed in the *Adi Granth*, which acquired for Sikhs the sanctity of the Moslems' Koran. Both alcohol and tobacco are forbidden in this basically most pacific of creeds.

The militancy which characterizes the Sikhs today developed only as Guru Nanak's successors got embroiled in national politics, with dire results for the Sikh community when their leaders challenged the Mughals. After the execution of Guru Tegh Bahadur in 1675, his son, Guru Gobind Singh, exalted the faithful henceforth to be constantly ready for armed defence of the faith. They were all to take the surname Singh, meaning "Lion" (all Sikhs are named Singh, but not all Singhs are Sikhs), and were to wear a turban and the five K's: *kesha* (uncut hair and beard), *kanga* (comb for their hair), *kara* (steel bracelet), *kachha* (soldier's shorts) and *kirpan* (dagger). Their distinctive appearance would make them highly visible and impose an unflinching courage.

Buddhism

It was founded over 2,500 years ago in reaction to Brahmanic orthodoxy and then practically vanished as an organized religion from the Indian scene by a process of persecution and absorption back into the Hindu mainstream. But Buddhism has continued to exert considerable influence on India's spiritual and artistic life to the present day.

Buddha's own life best explains his teachings but, like much of India's early centuries, the truth of that life is buried in legend and historical fact. According to a sprinkling of both, he was born Siddhartha Gautama in a grove of sal trees at Lumbini (due north of Varanasi just across the modern Nepalese border) around the year 566 B.C. His mother, queen of the Sakyas, is said to have conceived him after dreaming that a white elephant holding a lotus flower in his trunk had entered her side.

Siddhartha grew up in princely luxury. As a young man, he was

Sikkim's Tibetan monks reinforce Buddhism's comeback in India.

taken out one day to the edge of the royal parks where he saw for the first time the suffering of the poor, the sick and the aged. But he also saw a wandering religious beggar who alone seemed calm and serene. He realized the path his life must take.

Abandoning his riches, he went off into the kingdoms of the Ganga valley. For six years he begged for his food, learned to meditate and practised severe self-mortification, but still felt no nearer to understanding life's suffering. Then, aged 35, sitting crosslegged beneath a pipal tree at the place now known as Bodh Gaya (south of Patna), he vowed not to budge till he achieved his goal.

For 49 days he meditated, resisted the assaults of demons and temptresses, and became truly Enlightened—Buddha. He preached his new-found wisdom at Sarnath (near Varanasi). While an ever-growing band of disciples went out to spread his teachings, Buddha himself converted bandits and whole armies from the path of violence. In Kushinagar, between Bodh Gaya and his birthplace, he died aged 80, of dysentery, it is said, from eating pork.

Preaching that suffering came from the pursuit of individual desire, Buddha had advocated the Middle Way of the Eightfold Path: right views, right resolve, right speech, right conduct, right livelihood, right effort, right recollection and right meditation. Only thus could life's sorrows be overcome and the enlightenment of Nirvana be achieved.

This original doctrine without any sense of Buddha's divinity was embraced by the Hinayana (Lesser Vehicle) school which spread to Sri Lanka, Burma, Thailand, Cambodia and Laos. The Mahayana (Great Vehicle) school, adding the concept of Bodhisattva as a divine saviour, became the dominant form of Buddhism in India and spread across the Himalayas to China and Japan. After centuries of almost total eclipse in India, Buddhism has today achieved something of a renewal with the appeal to Hindu Untouchables for its egalitarian philosophy.

Jainism

As old as Buddhism, the Jain religion has made its mark with its elaboration of the concept of *ahimsa* or non-violence and is much more pacific than its name, which means religion of the conquerors.

Its founder, Vardhamana Mahavira, was born in 540 B.C. in Bihar and, like Buddha, was the son of a tribal chief. He, too, abandoned riches to become an ascetic. But unlike Buddha, Mahavira (Great Hero) pursued self-mortification to the end of his life,

even stripping off all his clothes to take his teachings naked from kingdom to kingdom in the Ganga valley. He died of self-starvation at 72 in the town of Para, near modern Rajgir. Later followers divided into the *Digambaras* ("space-clad", i.e. naked) and the *Svetambaras* ("white-clad") that you mostly see today.

The religion, in which Mahavira is in fact regarded as the last manifestation of 24 *Tirthankaras*

Jain non-violence protects the life of the humblest fly.

(teachers), attributes souls to all living creatures, as well as stones, water and other natural objects. Thus agriculture was abandoned for its inevitable destruction of plant and animal life. The ancient doctrines survive in strict vegetarianism, while Jain monks still carry feather dusters to sweep

57

insects gently away from where they tread and wear a gauze veil over their mouth to avoid breathing in a fly by accident.

Jainism never spread beyond India and today claims about 2 million followers, including many well-to-do businessmen in Gujarat and the Deccan, with a few in Bengal. It had considerable spiritual influence on the non-violent movement of Mahatma Gandhi, who used its fast-unto-death as a potent moral and political weapon.

Parsis, Jews and Christians

The Parsis, as their name suggests, originate from ancient Persia and are today only a minute community in the world of religions, with barely 100,000 in India, mostly in and around Bombay. But they have been and remain enormously influential in India's economic life and have often served as important go-betweens in the difficult relations between Hindus and Moslems, India and Pakistan.

Their religion dates back to the 7th century B.C. when their prophet Zoroaster contrasted his peaceful, sedentary People of Righteousness with the polytheistic nomadic People of Evil, an attitude that probably determined not only their ethics but also their occupational destiny as highly sophisticated businessmen. The Parsis base their elaborate code of ethics on the concept of a constant struggle between the forces of creation, light and good and those of darkness and evil, laying great emphasis on the purity of the natural elements, fire, earth and water. To avoid polluting the elements, they do not bury or cremate their dead but expose them naked on their famous Towers of Silence, for the vultures to devour.

India's Jewish and Christian communities are extremely old. Some texts claim that the first Jews came to India at the time of the Babylonian exile, in 587 B.C., others bring them to Cranganur, on the Malabar coast, in A.D. 72, about the same time that the apostle Thomas is said to have brought his Christian mission to India. The oldest remaining Jewish community is down the coast at Cochin (see p. 176), dating back at least to the 4th century A.D. Others, less orthodox, are to be found in Bombay, but most emigrated to Israel when it was founded in 1948.

The earliest Christians other than St. Thomas (see p. 188) were the Nestorian "heretics" of the Syrian Orthodox Church, also on the Malabar coast since the first centuries of the Christian era. Modern Christians are mainly Catholic in Goa, elsewhere all the British variations on Protestantism, each with a certain inescapable Hindu tinge to them.

WHERE TO GO

Where, indeed? This subcontinent is so huge, so rich and varied, that the choice of what to see, what to leave out on a first visit can be quite daunting. Don't even *think* of "doing" India the way people used to "do" Europe.

Unless you have several months at your disposal, you probably just wouldn't have the stamina to cover even a majority of the places of interest. But with some judicious selection from among the places we suggest, you can most certainly get a pretty good feel for the country in the three to four weeks that most people devote to a first trip.

However adventurous a spirit you are, with a taste for improvisation and a horror of schedules and detailed itineraries, you must accept from the outset, if your time is limited, that travelling around India demands a minimum amount of *planning*. Remember: there are over 750 million Indians out there and a lot of them are on the move at the same time as you, competing for plane seats and hotel rooms. So you will need to make at least some advance reservations for hotels in principal cities and especially for your major plane or train journeys. That can still leave you plenty of scope for getting off the beaten track and staying overnight in unexpected places.

Putting Together an Itinerary

We have divided the country up into five regions—north, west, centre, east and south.

In each of the regions, you'll find a major city like Delhi, Bombay or Madras which you can use as a starting-off point, also the best place for phoning home and making your other practical arrangements. Equally important, each area includes a place where, in the hallowed and eminently sensible military phrase, you can go for rest and recreation. In this case, you'll find a beach resort, nature reserve or one of the old hill-stations of the British Raj, each ideal for a change of pace or climate. It's easy to overdose on temples, palaces and museums. They are well worth your attention, but if you take plenty of time to relax as well as travel, you'll be surprised at how much more you can see and really appreciate.

If your budget allows you to fly around the country, you can compose a smorgasbord of places from each region, since you're not going to be able to do each exhaustively. In any case, we recommend that you choose from at least two of them, ideally three, when planning your "menu".

The Government of India Tourist Information Offices can be very helpful, both in your home country and on the spot. Their guides are usually much more reliable than those you might pick up outside the temples or palaces. But one word of warning: tour guides will give you a lot of contradictory explanations about the religious significance of this or that statue and many different versions of legend and historical "fact". It would be easy to dismiss them as a load of nonsense, but you'll understand India better if you appreciate that these explanations, at least in the religious domain, may all in their own way be *true*. When it comes to ideas (as opposed to personal interest), there's no more tolerant land on earth.

Practical Hints

The Berlitz-Info section at the back of the book gives you plenty of details on how to handle the practical side of your trip. But it's worth keeping a few general points in mind right now, when deciding where you're going in the time you have available.

The climate (see also p. 223) imposes its own imperatives and restrictions on your itinerary. Kashmir is impractical in December, Delhi unbearably hot in

Irrigation channels will bring desperately needed water to the parched earth.

*Visit the Fort at Agra in style,
in a maharaja's Palace on Wheels.*

June, trains to anywhere uncertain, to say the least, in the monsoon. Think just of three seasons: *cool*, *hot*, and *wet*, emphasized because they take on a special meaning in the Indian context.

From October to March, *cool*, except in the northern hills and mountains, where it's downright bitterly cold, means pleasantly warm by day, fresh enough for a sweater in the evening, at least until it starts hotting up by mid-February. This is the ideal season for seeing most of India.

From April to June, *hot* is prickly hot as most people have rarely experienced it, making the cities and plains in this season a bad bet, but the hill-stations and Kashmir are at their best.

Usually from mid-June to Sep-

Like a Maharaja

From the beginning of October to the end of March, Indian Railways organize one-week tours of Rajasthan (plus Agra and Delhi) on a train they call Palace on Wheels, *reproducing the luxury once enjoyed only by maharajas.*

The train takes you from Delhi to Jaipur, Udaipur, Jaisalmer, Jodhpur, Bharatpur, Agra and back to Delhi, with boat-cruises and rides on camels and elephants on the way. Book in advance from your travel agency before leaving home. It's not cheap, but then, that's what makes you feel like a maharaja.

tember, *wet* means monsoon wet, torrential rains, not all day every day, but often enough to make travel uncertain and mosquitoes and other bugs a nuisance. But the monsoon has its undoubted charms. The country is at its most luscious green and the temples and palaces, especially the Taj Mahal, take on an unmatchable glistening beauty. The wet season is also a great time to visit Kashmir, which has no monsoon.

With regard to your health (see also p. 228), two attitudes will guarantee you a miserable time: carelessness and hypochondria. Don't exaggerate in either direction. Take elementary precautions, sticking to bottled drinks and freshly cooked food, and you won't have any serious stomach problems. An occasional touch of Delhi belly is unavoidable when you're not used to the spicy food, but nothing to worry about. Just take it easy, drink plenty of liquids, and it'll pass. Admittedly, if you are on a short trip, you may need to take a quick-acting remedy to keep you on your feet, but in general, if you load up with antibiotics and a host of

63

other patent medicines, your body will never build up the necessary resistance and the next attack will just be worse.

One precaution is essential: protect yourself from the heat. Save your sun-tanning for the beach or the hotel swimming-pool, when you can cool off in the water. Otherwise, stay out of the sun. Wear a nicely ventilated hat and keep to the shady side of the street. Try to do your open-air sightseeing early in the morning and late afternoon. Take a siesta after lunch. Drink plenty of liquids—in the heat, dehydration is much more of a risk than an upset stomach.

In all senses of the word, stay cool. In the first few days, a combination of jet-lag, acclimatization and all-round culture shock may lead you to lose your temper when you see airports, railway stations and hotels not organized in a way you're used to. But don't forget, John Kenneth Galbraith called it *functioning* anarchy. Count to ten and, like Delhi belly, it'll pass. These days, airports, railway stations and hotels can be a pain anywhere. Indians are mostly a cheerful people and respond more readily to a smile than a scowl.

The red tape can at times seem like barbed wire, but that, too, can be handled. Part of India's legacy of several centuries of bureaucracy (don't just blame the British civil service, it began long before) is an inordinate respect for the written document and the rubber stamp. Don't knock it, use it. Vouchers, chits, passes, letters of introduction, printed business-cards, all work magic when you're faced with a "confirmed" reservation that suddenly becomes "unconfirmed".

If you're travelling by train (see p. 239) and rate peace of mind and personal comfort above the delights of adventurous improvisation, go first class with an *Indrail Pass*. It saves you interminable queues at the ticket office and gains you preferential treatment when it comes to reservations. Unless you're making several really long trips over a short period, Indian Airlines' *Discover India* ticket permitting 21 days of unlimited travel is financially less advantageous than individually purchased tickets, but buy these as far as possible *en bloc*, with confirmed reservations that you reconfirm on arrival at each new airport. A new computerized reservation system has been installed with the hope of making life easier.

Reverberating around every office you're likely to enter in India is one phrase calculated to make you tremble with fear, that cheerful prevarication: "No problem". If it rarely means what it says, you can at least interpret it as "no catastrophe" and go out and have a good time anyway.

THE NORTH

This is the major arena of Indian history. The region around Delhi includes the government capital and the heart of the old Mughal empire at Agra, but also the nature reserves of Corbett and Bharatpur. Up in the Himalayas, you'll find the refreshing hill-station of Simla, that served as the British summer capital, and the special magic of Kashmir.

DELHI

On the banks of the Yamuna (Jumna) river at the western end of the great Ganga valley, the nation's modern capital seems since earliest times to have occupied a coveted place for India's conquerors. Though they each very often destroyed much of the work of their predecessors, the 20th-century city remains a fascinating compendium of India's imperial history.

Recent archaeological findings suggest that a site on the west bank of the Yamuna river may have been the town of Indraprastha, home of the *Mahabharata* hero, King Yudhishthira, dating back to around 1000 B.C. A rock-inscription of Emperor Ashoka indicates Delhi was an important point on the trade route between the north-west frontier and Bengal in the 3rd century B.C.

The Tomara Rajputs made it their capital in 736, with the name of Dhillika, and it became a focus of clan-wars until the Moslems conquered it in 1193 and Qutb-ud-din Aybak set up his sultanate in 1206. The Rajputs' Delhi was dismantled to make way for the invaders' new monuments which in turn suffered from the devastating passage of Timur the Lame in 1398. He carried off not only 90 elephant-loads of building materials but also thousands of skilled Delhi stonemasons and sculptors to build his mosque at Samarkand. With the advent of the Mughals in 1526, Delhi alternated with Agra as capital, each ruler asserting himself with his own architectural caprices.

The town declined in importance with the eclipse of the Mughals, taking under the British a back seat to the more lucrative port-cities of Calcutta, Bombay and Madras until 1911, when it became once more a proud imperial capital. No less vain than the Mughals, the latest conquerors asserted their power by adding their own grandiose architectural caprices for the new seat of government, New Delhi, an amalgam of tributes to India's past but unmistakably British in overall conception.

Today, a tour of the capital takes you through an intriguing mixture of stately New Delhi's imposing ministries and embassies, modern office-blocks and luxury hotels along elegant avenues, and a bustling Old Delhi of vibrant Hindu and Moslem communities crowding in on the monuments of Mughal splendour. (For invaluable orientation, go to the Tourist Information Office on Janpath.)

Delhi of the Sultans

Start at the southern end of the city, with the **Qutb Minar**, an apt symbol of Islam's impact on India. Begun in 1199 by Delhi's first sultan, Qutb-ud-Din, and completed by his son-in-law Iltutmish, the 73-metre (240-ft.) red sandstone tower was erected to celebrate the Turkish conquest of Delhi and to cast "the shadow of God over the East and the West", with a muezzin at its top calling the faithful to prayer.

The tower achieves its elegance and power with the subtle differences in its four storeys, each a tapering cylinder varying the use of angular and convex ribs and separated by gracefully carved balconies, the top clad in marble.

In recent years, the top of the tower was popular for suicide pacts by young lovers refusing to accept arranged marriages. So it's now off-limits and the best bet for a panoramic view of the city is the top floor of one of the taller new hotels.

The mosque to which the tower's muezzin was calling the Moslem worshippers, now an impressive ruin, is the nearby **Quwwat-u'l-Islam-Masjid** ("The Might of Islam"). But it was built with the might of the Hindus. With little or no skilled Moslem labour at his disposal, Qutb called on the local craftsmen to build the mosque from the ruins of 27 of their own Hindu and Jain temples (demolished, into the bargain, by the labour of their elephants).

You can see the results of this collaboration in the colonnade of temple-pillars set one on top of the other. Sculptures of animals and deities have been effaced or plastered over, but the typically Indian intricate carving remains. Islamic architecture begins to come into its own with the five characteristic lofty peaked arches of the prayer-hall screen, but even there the decoration, including the Arabic lettering, is distinctly naturalistic and Hindu in style. The mosque is an object-lesson in Indian history: however powerful the conquerors, India's own particular genius has always shone through.

In the mosque's courtyard, you'll see a 7-metre-high (22-ft.) **Iron Pillar**, from the 4th-century Gupta period, according to its Sanskrit inscription, and brought here probably by the Rajput founders of Dhillika, but nobody knows where from. Amazingly unrusted after 1600 years of monsoon, this monument to the Hindu god Vishnu has special properties. If you stand with your back against it and completely encircle it with your arms—no mean feat—good luck is yours, at least for the rest of the day.

City of the Mughals

Almost due east of New Delhi's India Gate over by the Yamuna river, the much-plundered 16th-century **Purana Qila** (Old Fort) stands on an ancient mound, believed to mark the site of the city of Indraprastha of the *Mahabharata* epic.

As the earliest of Delhi's Mughal buildings, its mosque, the **Qal'a-i-Kuhna-Masjid**, with the minutely detailed moulding of its graceful peaked arches, represents an important transition from the Turco-Afghan to the more sophisticated style of the Persian-influenced Mughals. It was built in 1541 by Sher Shah, Emperor Babur's general who ruled northern India for five brief eventful years. **Sher-Mandal**, the two-storeyed red sandstone octagonal tower south of the mosque,

was the general's little pleasure-palace, but it proved to be the death of his rival and eventual successor, Humayun.

At least from this sad end came a splendid monument that you can see in the suburb of Nizamuddin, the **Tomb of Humayun**, built by his widow Haji Begum and recognized as the direct inspiration for Shahjahan's Taj Mahal at Agra. Drawing on the Koran's concept of heaven as a garden, the mausoleum is set back on a raised terrace in a lovely walled-in square of four tree-shaded lawns surrounded by hedges, though without the water that once ran in its channels ("rivers of life") and shallow rectangular pools that were to provide the perfect setting for the Taj.

Stone Cold Stoned

Everybody thought Emperor Humayun had kicked the opium habit when he got back from exile in Persia to reclaim his throne in 1555. But one day in the Sher-Mandal, which he had converted into a library to study books on astrology and puff a secret pipe or two, he was coming down the stairs, feeling more than a little woozy, when the muezzin started calling the faithful to prayer. The Great Mughal apparently tried to kneel right there on the staircase, tumbled over and cracked his head. Fatally.

But Humayun's Tomb has a remarkable charm of its own, a repose and serenity in the delicate combination of materials, buff and red sandstone with grey-trimmed white marble. With its majestic dome uniting four octagonal kiosks over the terrace-level's finely latticed arches, it's the first fully realized masterpiece of Mughal architecture. The six-pointed stars set in the abutments of the main arches are not the Jewish Star of David but an esoteric emblem that you'll see all over India.

Dominating Old Delhi, the grand **Red Fort** was built by Shahjahan in 1639 when he transferred the capital back to Delhi from Agra, drawing on his experience in remodelling Akbar's Fort there. Behind its good solid ramparts, the Delhi citadel, in keeping with the sensuous tastes of its builder, is more palace than fortress, preferring wherever possible white marble to the region's handsome but sometimes too omnipresent red sandstone. It's believed he used the same architect who collaborated with him on the Taj Mahal.

Coming from the south of the Fort's irregular octagonal oblong, notice outside the Delhi

Protesters at Delhi's Red Fort no longer risk a Mughal emperor sending out elephants to trample them.

Gate two monumental elephants. Part of the original design, they were destroyed by Emperor Aurangzeb, whose Islamic orthodoxy refused all images susceptible to idolatry. In the interests of architectural integrity, Viceroy Lord Curzon had these replicas reinstalled in 1903.

Enter the fort on its west side at the Lahore Gate. You find yourself immediately in a vaulted bazaar street, an idea Shahjahan borrowed from Baghdad, and still busy. Imagine the Mughal emperor's administrators and Rajput princes on elephants swaying through the arcade as far as the **Naqqar Khana** (Drum House), where the imperial band played five times a day and all visitors except the emperor and his closest relatives were obliged to dismount.

Pass with the ghosts of those nobles and commoners through the drum house to the **Diwan-i-Am** (Hall of Public Audience). There, beyond the cusped arches under a marble baldaquin supported by a statutory 40 pillars, the emperor sat cross-legged on the throne, "Seat of the Shadow of God". He held audience at noon, surrounded by nobles cordoned off in the hall by gold, silver or red velvet ropes, according to rank, while common petitioners attended in the courtyard below. As a privileged visitor, you can admire the inlaid stone panels of birds and flowers at the back of the hall.

Entrance to the **Diwan-i-Khas** (Hall of Private Audience) was for the privileged by ticket only. You'll find it just off to the left, among the palace apartments backing onto the Yamuna river. Beautiful as it still is with the delicately carved floral designs on the marble columns and cusped arches, imagine it in its glory before the ravages of Nadir Shah in 1739, whose Persian troops chipped the gold out of its pillars and the silver and gold inlay off the ceiling and then carted away the fabulous Peacock Throne. Above the corner arches of the north and south walls is the famous Persian inscription:

"If paradise on earth there be, 'Tis here, 'tis here, 'tis here!"
Last emperor to enjoy it was one George V, in 1911, for whom a painted wooden ceiling was installed.

One of the few palace apartments to survive is the principal harem, **Rang Mahal** (Palace of Colour). The walls' paintings have gone and water no longer flows in its indoor Nahr-i-Bihisht (River of Paradise), but mosaics of tiny mirrors still ornament the ceiling and walls of six boudoirs, sparkling a veritable little galaxy of stars when candle-lit. (If you don't have a guide with a candle, strike a match.) Southernmost of the palace buildings, **Mumtaz**

Mahal was also part of the imperial harem and is now a small museum of Mughal artwork.

North-west of the Diwan-i-Khas, the little **Moti Masjid** (Pearl Mosque)—its bulbous domes are actually of white and grey-veined marble—is the one contribution to the Fort by Shahjahan's pious successor, Aurangzeb, who used it as his private prayer-hall. (Each evening, a sound and light show at the Red Fort tells its story; details from the Tourist Information Bureau.)

Chandni Chowk, the road leading from the Fort's Lahore Gate, was once a grand avenue for imperial processions. Today, it is the main thoroughfare linking the most colourful of Delhi's bazaars, selling old gold, silver, pearls and jewellery, as well as clothes and traditional sweetmeats, in the narrow back-streets.

Standing on a high podium on an outcrop of rock south-west of the Red Fort, Shahjahan's other great construction for his capital, the **Jama Masjid** (the great congregational "Friday Mosque"), is the largest mosque in India. The advisability of an early morning or late afternoon visit on hot days becomes apparent when you contemplate the mosque's three formidable pyramidal flights of steps up to the gate-houses. The 100-square-metre (1,076-sq.-ft.) courtyard at the top is enclosed by the cloistered shade of long arched colonnades with a stone-canopied pavilion at each corner.

The sandstone prayer hall highlights the emperor-builder's almost feminine aesthetic sense in the lotus calyx on the gateway's two lantern shafts, the delicately flaring balconies on the minarets, and the curving stripes to emphasize the onion-quality of the three bulbous marble domes.

Far in spirit from the Mughals but an integral part of Old Delhi, is **Raj Ghat**, the simple memorial to Mahatma Gandhi overlooking the Yamuna river south of the Red Fort. On lawns planted with

---

Victorian Vandals

Mongols and Persians weren't the only plunderers to hit Delhi. Most of the Red Fort's palace apartments were dismantled by the British to build army barracks after recapturing the city from the mutineers in 1857. This officially sanctioned vandalism has to be understood in the vindictive climate that reigned after the mutiny. Amends were made by the enlightened viceroys who were the first of India's foreign rulers to protect and restore its cultural patrimony. But Lord Curzon and company frequently had to combat philistine circuit judges, who thought nothing of whitewashing or plastering over frescoes in a Mughal mausoleum while turning it into a rest-house.

trees donated by visiting heads of state, this square platform of black marble marks the spot where Gandhi was cremated in 1948. A museum records the highlights of his life. The platform's only inscription records his last words, *Hé Ram* (Oh, God). Nearby, a sign proclaims the so-called Gandhi Talisman: "Recall the face of the poorest and most helpless man whom you may have seen and ask yourself if the step you contemplate is going to be of any help to him."

New Delhi

Nostalgics of the British Empire will miss the old street-names. Clive Road is now Tyagraja, Queen Victoria Road has become Rajendra Prasad, Curzon is Kasturba Gandhi, but who laments the passing of such prosaic names as Circular (now Nehru) or Over Bridge (now Desh Bandhu Gupta)?

Though the statues of kings and queens, viceroys and generals have also disappeared, the British spirit remains in the city's planning. In keeping with the colonial policy of separating the British cantonment from the Indian quarters with the barrier of a railway, the new city built for the

British Empire's Indian seat of government is separated from Old Delhi by the line running from Amritsar to Agra. (Old Delhi railway station, complete with funny little turrets, looks like a British version of the Red Fort.)

The monumental British Neoclassic sandstone architecture mixes more or less happily with elements of the Buddhist, Hindu and Mughal past and the sweep-

India Gate presents a proud but hazy memory of the British Raj.

ing geometry of its plan exudes the ineffable self-confidence of empire. As a visiting statesman once said of the government complex: "What splendid ruins it will make!"

The commercial pivot of New Delhi is the circular shopping-arcade and bustling roundabout of **Connaught Place**. Surrounded by cinemas, banks, travel agencies, high-class restaurants and the better craft emporiums, it's one place where the new Indian name, Indra Chowk, does not seem to catch on.

Connaught Place straddles the north-east/south-west axis linking the Jama Masjid mosque of Old Delhi to India's parliament, **Sansad Bhavan**. Designed by Herbert Baker, the rather too massive colonnaded rotunda of the parliament building is at its best illumi-

nated at night with a silhouette of light-bulbs.

More successful is Edwin Lutyens' Viceroy's Residence, now the president's house, **Rashtrapati Bhavan**. With its four wings radiating from the imposing grey-blue dome of the central block and the geometric pools and lawns of its magnificent gardens, it achieves something of the grandeur of Britain's heyday. From its artifi-

cial hill it looks down along the great processional avenue, Rajpath (once Kingsway), flanked by parklands, where India holds its military march-pasts on Republic Day, January 26. At the other end of Rajpath stands **India Gate**, the war memorial to 90,000 Indian

Tattoos for festive occasions are decorative but not indelible.

Army soldiers who died in World War I, designed by Lutyens in the style of a triumphal arch.

One of the city's strangest monuments, geographically in New Delhi south of Connaught Place but historically in that nebulous 18th century of the Mughals' decline when the city was up for grabs to any passing adventurer, is the **Jantar Mantar**. Difficult to believe that this bizarre collection of geometrical shapes, staircases going nowhere and windows in walls without rooms behind them, was built in 1724 by a serious student of the heavens rather than in the 20th century by some deranged architect hit on the head by one of his son's building-blocks.

It's in fact the astrologico-astronomical observatory of Rajput prince Jai Singh II from Jaipur (see p. 101), where he built another, as well as three others in Ujjain, Varanasi and Mathura. The centrepiece is the Samrat Yantra (Supreme Instrument), a right-angled triangle, with a nice domed viewing canopy at the top, that acts as a gigantic sun dial, claimed to be "accurate to half a second". The hypotenuse, you see, is parallel to the earth's axis.

Nearby, of no historical or architectural importance, but probably the liveliest Hindu temple in the city, is the **Hanuman Mandir** (Temple of the Monkey God), a jolly theatre of age-old supersti-tion where you can get acquainted with the joyous atmosphere of popular Hinduism. Hanuman is a beloved, most beneficent deity, predating classical Hinduism, and the reason why no one would dream of harming the langur, the grey-furred, black-faced little monkey you'll see scampering around everywhere.

Museums

In what is artistically a predominantly Mughal city, the **National Museum**, on Janpath (Queensway) south of Rajpath, is worth visiting for its collection of old Hindu sculpture, particularly from the medieval southern India of the Vijayanagar kingdom.

Railway buffs will enjoy the display of India's earliest steam engines at the open-air **Rail Transport Museum** in the diplomatic neighbourhood of Chanakyapuri (behind the Bhutan Embassy). Adventurous as rail travel in India still is, one intriguing exhibit belongs, we hope, firmly in the past: the skull of an elephant that tried to derail a mail train in 1894.

The **Nehru Memorial Museum**, devoted to the life of India's first prime minister and the fight for Independence, is located in the house which Nehru inherited from the British Indian Army Commander-in-Chief on Teen Murti Road (sound and light shows in the evenings).

AGRA

Because of its Taj Mahal, Agra is undoubtedly the most popular sightseeing destination in India. Even if it had nothing else, it would be worth the trip, for the Taj, as you soon learn to call it affectionately, is a "sight" that awakens the wonder and enthusiasm of the most blasé, world-weary traveller.

Getting There—and Back

Unless it's unavoidable, don't try to do Agra in one day. It's possible (and certainly better than missing it), but it means you won't be able comfortably to see much more than the Taj and, say, the Fort. More important, you might miss the unique beauty of the Taj changing in the light of different times of day.

If you are in a hurry, there's a flight down from Delhi, but an air-conditioned first-class seat on the Taj Express (3 hours) makes a pleasant introduction to the adventure of Indian railways. If you go by car, try to avoid returning to Delhi after dark. The heavy commercial traffic, with goats and cows not wearing head-lights, is a risk for the most disciplined chauffeur.

Alternatively, Agra is a stop on the Indian Railways luxury train Palace on Wheels (see p. 63).

As it is, there's plenty more. Agra was the capital of Akbar the Great, the site of his fort, of his tomb outside the city at Sikandra and, a few miles west at Fatehpur Sikri, of the marvellous deserted town he built to celebrate the birth of a son and which he abandoned to fight on the north-west frontier. And heirs of the craftsmen brought here to build the Mughals' proudest monuments continue a tradition in jewellery, brassware, carved ivory and inlaid marble.

The first we really hear of Agra is when Sultan Sikandar Lodi made it his capital in 1501. Babur captured it in 1526 and, with it, the Koh-i-Nur diamond that ended up in the British crown jewels. His grandson Akbar chose Agra for his capital rather than Delhi, which he found too full of crude Afghans. In the 17th century, Jahangir made it a major cultural focus of the Islamic world, with a population of over half a million (today, around 750,000).

His son Shahjahan progressively lost his taste for Agra after completing the mausoleum for his beloved wife, Mumtaz-Mahal. He moved the capital back to Delhi in 1648, leaving the treasures of Agra to the vandals (including the British after the 1857 Mutiny) until the viceroys organized the restoration. Today, it is pollution which is taking its toll on Agra's monuments.

Taj Mahal

This is truly a monument for all seasons. There are those who swear by *Sharad Purnima*, the first full moon after the monsoons, a cloudless midnight in October, when the light is at its clearest, its most romantic. Others love to see it right in the middle of the heaviest monsoon, its marble seemingly translucent, the reflected image blurred in the rain-stippled water-channels of the garden. But its magic is strong at any time of year, and any moment of the day. At dawn, its colour changes from milk to silver to rose-pink. At sunset, it is golden. But see it, too, in the brilliance of midday, for then it is utterly, dazzlingly *white*. On the days of the full moon, the grounds stay open till midnight.

The red sandstone vaulted **gateway** to the gardens of the mausoleum would in any other setting be admired as a masterpiece in its own right, with its noble marble-framed arches, the domed kiosks on the four corner turrets and two rows of 11 small *chhatri* (umbrella-domes) atop the entrance. As it is, it provides the perfect frame for your first view (and photo?) of the ensemble. Long-range photography is allowed, but it is forbidden to take pictures inside the monument.

The classical *chharbagh* (four-square) **gardens** are, of course, an integral part of the Taj Mahal, spiritually as the symbol of the paradise to which Mumtaz-Mahal has ascended and artistically to enhance the perspective, colour and texture of the mausoleum. The dark cypresses heighten the brilliance of the monument's marble, and the shallow water-channels, meeting at a broad cen-

---

A Marble Requiem

Mahal means palace, but in this case Taj Mahal is a diminutive of the name Mumtaz-Mahal ("Exalted of the Palace") which Shahjahan's cousin received when she married him. Daughter of his mother's brother, she had been his constant companion long before he succeeded to the throne and then truly a "first lady" among the hundreds in his harem. In 19 years of marriage, she bore him 14 children, dying with the birth of the last, in 1631.

Shahjahan's beard—he was 39, one year older than his wife —turned white practically overnight and he continued to mourn for years, dressing in white on each anniversary of her death. The 12 years taken to build her mausoleum, working untiringly with his Persian architect and with craftsmen brought from Baghdad, Italy and France, may be regarded as the supreme sublimation of his grief. "Empire has no sweetness," he wrote, "for me now, life itself has lost all relish."

tral viewing-platform, not only provide a perfect second image but also, with the reflection of the sky, add at dawn and sunset a subtle illumination from below.

Exquisite harmony and refined symmetry are the keynotes of the **mausoleum** itself. The whole of

the central structure is clad in miraculously white marble (from the Rajasthan quarries of Makrana), achieving a magnificent texture with the subtly alternating broad and narrow slabs. Standing protectively at the four corners of the raised terrace, the minarets are deferentially just slightly lower than the sublime central cupola. The octagonal cenotaph-chamber contains the ceremonial

The Taj Mahal—exquisite elegy in marble, eternally enchanting.

marble coffins of both Mumtaz-Mahal and Shahjahan while, as was the custom, the bodies are entombed in another chamber directly below.

You'll need a candle or pocket-torch in the cenotaph-chamber as daylight now barely filters through the beautiful marble trellis-screens (they were conceived before glass had to be added to keep out the birds). True roman-tics may not regret the vandals' removal of the tomb's more spectacular treasures, as they left the gentler, subdued beauty of the ornamental roses and poppies in the inlay of semi-precious stones (black and white onyx, green chrysolite, red carnelian and variegated agate).

The mausoleum is flanked by two almost identical red sandstone buildings, to the west a

mosque, to the east a guest-pavilion, each making a perfect viewing-point. Try the pavilion at sunrise and the mosque at sunset. But go round the back of the Taj, too, to the broad terrace overlooking the Yamuna river, with a view as far as the Agra fort.

The Agra Fort

Built by Akbar in 1565, at a more embattled period than Shahjahan's Red Fort in Delhi, it was conceived as a classical fortified citadel, also in red sandstone, with a moat on three sides and the Yamuna river on the fourth. Pleasure palaces were a secondary consideration and indeed mostly additions by Akbar's successors.

The entrance from the south, at Amar Singh Gate, takes you up a ridged elephant's ramp deliberately sloped to slow down potential attackers. Pass into the great quadrangle of the long, sandstone-pillared **Diwan-i-Am** (Hall of Public Audience) where the only petitioners left are the wild green parakeets in the trees. It was in this courtyard in 1609 that Captain William Hawkins began Britain's long association with India's rulers by presenting to Emperor Jahangir a letter of introduction from King James I.

North of the quadrangle is Shahjahan's handsome **Moti Masjid** (Pearl Mosque), built up on sloping ground with a marble-cloistered courtyard and marble pool in the centre. Climb the narrow staircase to the roof of the mosque for a fine view of the fort as a whole.

Off the north-east corner of the Diwan-i-Am, the royal ladies of the harem had their own mosque, **Nagina Masjid**, and Hindu temple, and between the two their own little bazaar, a courtyard where merchants were invited in to sell their silks, jewels and trinkets. Around the corner, beside the *hammam* (baths), the **Diwan-i-Khas** (Hall of Private Audience) is decorated with superb carving and inlaid white marble. The crack in Jahangir's marble throne came from a British cannonball in 1857. As in Delhi's Fort, most of the private palace apartments face the Yamuna river. Among the most charming are the arcaded loggia and gilt-roofed pavilions of the **Khas Mahal** or Private Palace.

A tiny staircase took the emperor up to the **Musamman Burj**, the pretty pavilion of his chief wife, directly overlooking the river. It is also popularly known as "Prisoner's Tower" as it was here that Aurangzeb shut up his father Shahjahan, graciously allowing him for his last days a stunning view of his Taj Mahal.

The **Palace of Jahangir** (actually built by Akbar, but embellished by his son) is constructed around a square court with elegant arches along the upper gallery. There's a distinctly Hindu flavour to the decoration of the ceiling in the main hall—snakes shooting out of the mouths of elephants. In a small hall on the west side, you'll see peacocks holding snakes in their beaks.

Other Sights

On the opposite bank of the Yamuna from the fort is the lovely **Tomb of Itimad-ud-Daulah**, too often ignored because it was subsequently overshadowed by the Taj. It was built some 15 years earlier by Jahangir's wife, Nur Jahan, for her Persian-born father, who served as Mughal prime minister. There's a delicate, almost fragile elegance to the white marble pavilion's graceful silhouette, with its squared cupola and four octagonal turrets, topped by domed kiosks. The lattice-work on the arches and windows is superb, but its outstanding feature is the exquisite marble inlay—geometric patterns outside and wine-flasks, goblets and flower-vases around the cenotaph. This decoration is even more abundant than in the Taj and, thanks to the vandals' oversight, better preserved.

Akbar's pink sandstone and white marble mausoleum, at **Sikandra**, is 10 kilometres (6 mi.) north of Agra. The best view is from the top of the great gateway. On the cenotaph are inscribed the 99 names of Allah.

Fatehpur Sikri

In a country of crowded cities, it makes a refreshing change to go 37 kilometres (22 mi.) south-west of Agra to a rocky outcrop on which stands the deserted citadel of Fatehpur Sikri that Akbar, on a whim, briefly made his imperial capital.

Fatehpur, planned as a cultural, commercial and administrative capital with nearby Agra as a fallback position in case of attack, is nonetheless protected on three sides by a system of ramparts measuring about 6 kilometres (4 mi.). On the fourth side is a long, artificial lake stretching 8 kilometres (5 mi.) to the Rajasthan border, never sufficient, apparently, for the needs of the citadel and so one of the probable reasons why Akbar did not settle here permanently.

The citadel was built by some of the architects working on the Agra Fort and adds to the predominant pink sandstone the darker red stone of the mountain-ridge.

You enter through the **Agra Gate**, at the north-east corner, passing on the right the *karkhanas* (workshops) where stone-masons, carpenters and weavers provided for the court's daily needs.

In the **Diwan Khana-i-Am**, the great courtyard for public audiences, Akbar dispensed his justice accompanied by an executioner with his instruments of torture

*Akbar's capital is deserted,
but merchants still do good business.*

and death. They weren't actually used then and there, but the sight of them was felt to serve as a very effective means of getting at the truth, the whole truth and nothing but the truth. At the foot of the colonnade opposite the emperor's pavilion, you'll see a big stone tethering-ring for an elephant whose job it was to crush to death the occasional capital criminal.

Go through the pavilion to the **Daulat Khana** (Abode of Fortune, the imperial palace) on the south side of the courtyard. Epitomizing Akbar's efforts to unite his Hindu subjects with their Islamic conquerors, the striking feature of the palace is the strong Hindu character of the decoration: col-

panel and pillar creates an illusion of woodwork rather than stone.

More than India's other imperial residences, Fatehpur is subject to colourful stories in which it isn't always possible to establish a historian's "truth". For instance, in the middle of the courtyard is the **Pachisi Court**, a giant-sized sort of chessboard for the game of *pachisi*, where Akbar and pals are believed to have used human "pieces"—each player moving around a team of four slave-girls in different coloured costumes. Why not?

To the **Astrologer's Pavilion**, in the north-west corner of the court, Akbar is said to have come for a daily dose of forecasts from the house-esoteric. The emperor is known to have in fact consulted, elsewhere, a whole panel of experts of the Hindu and Moslem schools of astrology. Behind it is the **Treasury Pavilion**, where you can imagine him, keen administrator that he was, seated on cushions under the lovely arches curving like outstretched elephant trunks, watching the counting of the imperial money. But better, and perhaps erroneously, the building was also known as Ankh Michauli (Blind Man's Buff). Here, Akbar was thought to have sported with his wives, hiding and seeking behind the great square pillars. Was this the sport of such a serious empire-builder?

umns with elaborately carved bell-shaped pedestals and stylized elephant heads forming the capitals; most beautiful of all, the sculpted stone screens and intricate chiselling in the stone walls to imitate painting.

In the south-east corner of the courtyard, the **Turkish Sultana's House**, or Hujra-i-Anup Talao (Chamber of the Peerless Pool), the fine detail of the apes, pheasants and lions covering every wall

Most hotly disputed of all is the purpose of the so-called **Diwan-i-Khas**, not necessarily the hall of private audience that this implies. It's dominated by one great central pillar supporting on its massive, intricately carved capital a criss-cross of bridges to an upper balcony. Some claim it was here that Akbar held his famous debates with Jesuits, Brahmans, Parsi Zoroastrians, Sufi mystics, Jain and Buddhist monks, the sages arguing below while the emperor sat listening, invisible atop his pillar, or strode around the bridges and balcony hurling down his awkward questions. Others insist that it was just a storehouse for jewels. Truth in India, even more than beauty, is in the eye of the beholder.

Walk across the courtyard to the beautiful five-tiered **Panch Mahal**, a palace with the delightful Persian system of ventilation known as *badgir* (wind-tower). It's without walls on three sides, open for the breezes to sweep in from top to bottom. Each floor is supported on columns that diminish in number from 84 at ground-level to just four for the pavilion on the roof. Notice that no two of the meticulously carved columns on the ground floor are exactly alike. Be careful with the steep climb to the top, but it's well worth it for the wonderful **view** across the whole citadel, particularly the palaces of the Imperial Harem to the southwest.

The Harem's principal residence is **Jodh Bai's Palace**, built for Akbar's Hindu wife, the first royal spouse not to be required to convert to her husband's Islamic faith. It was Akbar's favourite

---

Where Did You Go, Akbar?

The rise and fall of Fatehpur Sikri is the perfect illustration of Akbar's impulsive personality. At the end of 1568, the emperor was 26 and still without a male heir. At Sikri he met a Sufi mystic, Shaikh Salim Chishti, who promised him, given the proper spiritual dedication, not one, but three sons.

"In return for your friendship and grace," said the emperor, "I'll protect and preserve you."

Not overawed, the Sufi replied: "You can name your first son after me."

The following August, a boy was born. He was duly named Salim (later Jahangir). Overjoyed, Akbar decided to move his capital to Sikri, then went off on a successful military campaign and came back to add the name of Fatehpur (City of Victory).

By 1581 he abandoned Fatehpur. Only the family of Shaikh Salim Chishti remained, near the shrine Akbar had built for them. Today, 16 generations later, they're still there, but no more sign of Akbar's people.

---

residence at Fatehpur. The palace has one side screening out the summer heat while the other is open to the cooler breezes. Its most cherished feature is the turquoise glazed ceramic tiling of the roof of the north and south wings.

Fatehpur's **Jama Masjid** (Friday Mosque), at the southern end of the citadel on top of its mountain-ridge, was the first of the great open courtyard mosques that became characteristic of all Mughal cities. Notice the splendidly carved central *mihrab* (the recess marking the direction of Mecca). The gleaming white jewel of the red sandstone courtyard is the marble-clad **Tomb of Shaikh Salim Chishti**, who died at 92. The tomb's façade is handsomely inscribed with black calligraphy, the cenotaph-chamber decorated with delicately painted flowers. This was originally a much simpler sandstone monument, its marble skin being the addition of a grateful Jahangir who, without Shaikh Salim Chishti, might never have seen the light of day.

Bharatpur

Strictly speaking, Bharatpur is in Rajasthan, but its easy accessibility 42 kilometres (26 mi.) west of Agra makes it more logical to include it here. The lakes and marshlands of the bird sanctuary of the **Keoladeo-Ghana** offer an excellent change of pace. Even if you're not a fanatical bird-watcher, you'll enjoy the walks and drives through the woodland, with the chance of seeing herds of nilghai antelope, blackbuck and cheetal (spotted deer). A good time of year to visit is at the end of the monsoon in October, when there are huge colonies of storks.

Harems, the Cold Facts

The Indian Moslems' purdah that strictly separated women behind a screen in special apartments, derived from the old Persian institution of the harem. Armed security guards inside the harem were all female, no men, except for eunuchs at the outside doors.

In Akbar's time, women were admitted to the harem as an honour to their families, an imperial favour to some politically useful noble, certainly not always nor even very often for the emperor's sexual pleasure. Though he might have several hundred "wives", very few were his regular companions.

The senior wife, mistress of the household, was a person of great influence in the realm, guardian of one of the two imperial seals needed to authorize a new statute, the emperor's confidante in many of his decisions. the most famous example was Mumtaz-Mahal, wife of Shahjahan, but much more powerful was Jahangir's wife, Nur Jahan, who practically ran the whole country.

---

herons, egrets and cormorants. This is ideally combined with a full-moon trip to the Taj, but there's plenty to see all year round.

Among more than 300 species spotted here, you'll find eagles, cranes, pelicans, snakebirds, kingfishers and a host of ducks and geese, as well as a flock of rare wintering Siberian cranes between January and March.

The Maharaja of Bharatpur organized annual duck-shoots here for British viceroys and other top officials as well as fellow princes—a slaughter of thousands. Nowadays hunting is completely banned. Bharatpur is for the birds.

This cat has nine lives. You have only one, so keep your distance.

CORBETT PARK

Among India's many nature reserves, this is probably the best known because of the audacious hunter of the man-eating tigers of Kumaon, Jim Corbett. The park was established in 1935 and was given Corbett's name after India became independent.

North-east of Delhi, this lovely park of forest and meadows along the Ramganga river in the foothills of the Himalayas is still the home of tiger, leopard and elephant, as well as cheetal, sloth bear, wild pig, jackal and hyena. The river is stocked with mahseer and trout, an occasional blind freshwater dolphin and two kinds of crocodile. Bird-watchers look out for stork, red jungle-fowl and black partridge.

The forest is thick with sissoo and tall sal trees, both much prized for their timber for ship-building and sleepers (ties) for railway tracks. The great joy is an elephant-ride, swinging through the jungle and grassland reclining on your cushioned howdah. Rest at midday in the lodge at Dhikala and watch from the verandah a herd of elephant heading down to the river.

Be sure to plan ahead through the Tourist Information Office or a Delhi travel agency. Admission to the park is by permit only, easy to obtain, with reserved accommodation either in the lodges or the official camping-grounds.

CHANDIGARH

The capital of the Punjab* is a stopover on your way to Simla or, if you cannot get a seat on the heavily booked non-stop flights from Delhi or Bombay to Srinagar, a half-way stage on the journey to Kashmir. In either case, it's worth spending at least a few hours visiting this unique modern city planned from scratch in 1950 by the great Swiss-French architect Le Corbusier.

Architecture-buffs and urbanists may want to make a special trip, anyway. Corbu, as colleagues called this eccentric revolutionary of modern design, was invited by the Indian government to create an entirely new city for the post-Partition Punjab on a windy plain at the foot of the Himalayas.

With his British associate Maxwell Fry designing most of the bright, colourful housing, Corbu created the major public buildings and laid out a town of spacious boulevards and sweeping tree-lined avenues, inspired by some of Lutyens' ideas for New Delhi but, so far, blessedly uncongested by the growing traffic.

*At the time of going to press, the Sikhs' holy city of Amritsar and its Golden Temple seemed likely to remain off limits to foreign tourists for the foreseeable future. But you can get a good idea of Sikh architecture and its forms of worship at one of their other great national shrines, the Har Mandir Takht in Patna (see p.161).

He planned the town on the principle of the human body, with the government buildings of the **Capitol** and university at the head, the heart being the commercial town-centre (a pedestrian zone), and the arms and legs being the industrial districts.

In the Capitol's square **Assembly** building for the state parliament, the long **Secretariat** administrative block, the great vaulted

High Court and the smaller **Governor's Residence**, you can see the master's signature in his use of huge slabs of brute concrete as if it were weathered granite from the nearby mountains. With none of the British nostalgia for the Hindu or Mughal past, the buildings achieve their power by varying geometric with amorphous shapes, but soften the crude force of the concrete in the High Court,

for example, with bright pastel blues, vermilions and lemon yellows behind the sun-breaker grilles.

A playful side to this very deliberate, but not heartless urban planning can be enjoyed with a walk through the nearby **Rock Garden** of higgledy-piggledy concrete blocks. East of the Capitol, take a row-boat out on the artificial **Sukhna Lake**.

SIMLA

Like Chandigarh, this town, now capital of the state of Himachal Pradesh, was created from scratch, back in the early 19th century when the British were looking around desperately for

Chandigarh's modern tapestries, a Punjabi pipe-dream?

refuges from the heat of the plains.

At an altitude of 2,130 metres (6,755 ft.), it was once just a spot where a religious ascetic offered cool spring-water to thirsty travellers coming out of the Himalayas. Some of them were British troops fresh from their war with the Gurkhas of Nepal in 1819. They came back to build mountain retreats, not chalets, but regular little cottages or an occasional grander mansion. From 1832, when Lord William Bentinck, the governor-general, spent a very happy summer here, it became the most prestigious of all hill-stations. The viceroys made it their summer capital, right down to Lord Mountbatten, who pondered the last details of Independence and Partition here in 1947.

The old reasons to head for the hills make a trip to Simla still more than valid, even if the old viceregal glamour has gone. The air is sweet, cool and clear and the pleasure of the quaint English village atmosphere remains, along with some lovely walks into the surrounding mountains. (Get acclimatized to the altitude before attempting any long hikes.)

In town, retrace the favourite promenades along the shops of the **Mall** and the old administrative offices of the **Ridge**. Where the two meet was what Kipling called "Scandal Point". At the eastern end of the Mall is the little **Gaiety Theatre**, old home of the Simla Amateur Dramatic Company and its programmes of Victorian melodrama and Edwardian operetta.

High Jinks in the Hills

The British established hill-stations wherever they could find a bit of reasonably accessible altitude—for Madras, Ootacamund (Ooty) in the Nilgiri Hills, for Bombay, Mahabaleshwar in the Western Ghats, and for Delhi and Calcutta, there was a choice in the Himalayas of Simla, Mussoorie, Darjeeling, and many more. In the general relief at escaping the hell of the summerheat, they managed, in the classical British manner, to be very proper on the surface and nicely naughty underneath.

In these last bastions of the British Raj, class inevitably reared its pretty head, the hillstations, like seaside resorts back home, each having its own cachet. Senior officers made so-called "poodle-faking stations" off limits to subalterns, not permitted to watch their superiors poodle-faking with other men's wives. For, as Rudyard Kipling put it,

"Jack's own Jill goes up the hill
To Muree or Chakrata.
Jack remains and dies in the plains
And Jill remarries soon after."

The Ridge takes you past the neo-Gothic Anglican **Christ Church**, where the bells are made from the brass of cannons captured from the Sikhs. At the end of the Ridge, beyond the old Cecil Hotel, you'll find the lofty baronial pile of **Viceregal Lodge**, now used by the Institute for Advanced Studies. In the neatly tailored grounds of the ivy-covered greystone mansion, you can still imagine the rickshaws pulling up

Not unusual to see the ladies doing the heavy work, with a smile.

at the porch for one of the viceroy's banquets. Peek inside at the teak-panelled hall with its great fireplace, coffered ceiling and majestic staircase. Can you hear *Rule Britannia*? Continue up to the top of **Jakko Hill** for a fine view of the town and the plunging valley.

KASHMIR

The Vale of Kashmir, 1,700 metres (5,000 ft.) above sea level, is one of those dream worlds, not just for the modern tourist, but of all time for the many conquerors who have passed through the deserts of Sind and the hot and dusty plains of the Ganga valley and heard tell of its blessed meadows, forests, fruit orchards and lakes. It remains the disputed treasure of the subcontinent.

Planning Your Kashmir Stay

Many people, particularly in high summer, make Kashmir the principal destination of their visit to India, combining it with perhaps just brief side trips in Delhi and Agra. But if you're making a wider tour of India, it's a good idea to plan Kashmir for the end, when you can relax on a houseboat on a lake or go on a refreshing hike in the surrounding mountains.

The Himalayas are a heady site for skiing. Down in the valley they grow yellow colza for its oil.

In any case, for Kashmir more than anywhere else in India, it is truly imperative that you arrange your travel and accommodation well in advance. In the holiday season, Srinagar flights are always heavily booked, so be sure to arrive in India with confirmed reservations for the return, too. Your travel agency can reserve you a houseboat, at least for a couple of days, allowing you to change around once you're settled in. One important advantage of advance reservations is that you'll be met at the airport by a representative of the houseboat owner—it's not easy to find your own way among the boats.

93

KASHMIR

You may, of course, prefer a hotel to a houseboat, but it would be a pity to miss this beautifully preserved relic of the heyday of the British Raj. In the 19th century, when Kashmir offered the most exotic hill-station of them all, the maharaja forbade the British to buy land there, so they hit on the brilliant alternative of building luxuriously appointed houseboats moored on the lakes around Srinagar. Equipped with all the Victorian upper middle class comforts, the more manoeuvrable smaller houseboats made their way to other lakes for duck-shoots or just for the pleasures of the cruise, while the larger ones stayed put.

Today, with many new boats built in the same old style, with beautiful Kashmiri wood-carving along the bridge and decks, most

are too heavy to move around. But the traditional comforts are the same, old-fashioned wood-burning stoves, plush armchairs in the living room, warm carpeting in two or three spacious bedrooms with, in most cases, superb personal service and fine Kash-

A little shikara *plies its way among the houseboats on Dal Lake.*

miri cuisine. Dine out on deck. You arrange with the owner what you want to eat each day, Western or Indian style.

Most houseboats are moored on Dal Lake, but if you're seeking seclusion, there are others on the smaller Nagin Lake to the west. They are serviced by *shikaras*, gaily decorated roofed canoes somewhat reminiscent of Venetian gondolas, that ply their way around the lake, ferrying passengers, but also a veritable floating market of fruit, vegetables and flowers, with a flourishing, not very clandestine trade in marijuana. The *shikaras* also bring to your deck a plethora of carpets, silks, cashmere shawls, brassware, jewels, wood-carvings, even the services of tailors with fanciful names like Savile Roy to recall their old British allegiance.

Srinagar

The heart of Kashmir's capital is built along the serpentine Jhelum river on the southern shore of the lakes. Even if you don't intend to buy, the bazaars, tailor's shops and government emporiums (one of them, the handsome old British Residency) are fascinating places to observe the style and gall of that special breed, the charming but often quite shameless scoundrel, the Kashmiri merchant.

Few old monuments have survived Kashmir's troubled history,

but the city's beauty is in its lakes and gardens.

Take plenty of time for a leisurely cruise around **Dal Lake** and the adjoining **Nagin**, lounging on the cushions of a *shikara*. You coast under weeping willows, out past the fishermen, and among the lovely **floating gardens** that grow melons, tomatoes, cucumbers and white lotus root in a mesh of reeds and mud floating in

---

Beautiful Bone of Contention
Alexander left Greek settlements guarding the western frontiers of Kashmir and other Greeks filtered into the mountain-kingdom to account perhaps for the blue eyes and red hair of many Kashmiris today. In the 3rd century B.C., Emperor Ashoka is said to have sent his Buddhist missionaries to found the town of Srinagar.

In medieval times, Kashmir remained, with a brief Mongol interlude, under Hindu kings until Afghans conquered it for Islam in the 14th century. With their equal enthusiasm for iconoclasm and creativity, they smashed the Hindu temples and introduced the arts of silk-weaving, shawl-embroidery, wood carving and ornamental papier-mâché that have been the glory of Kashmir ever since.

Kashmir flourished under the Mughals, Akbar appreciating the sweet fruits of its orchards that he missed in the plains, Jahangir and Shahjahan laying out gardens that provoked the envy of Louis XIV when he heard about them. The Persian plunderer, Nadir Shah, couldn't resist laying claim to Kashmir but was soon replaced again by the Afghans. Supreme indignity for the Moslems came with the Sikh conquest led by Ranjit Singh in 1819.

The British did not help matters much nearly 30 years later when they took the state away from the Sikhs and handed it to a Hindu Rajput prince, under British protection, with Moslems forming an overwhelming majority of the population (today 68%). Moslem invaders tried to overthrow the Hindu ruler in 1947 and the latter, Maharaja Hari Singh, was rescued by the Indian Army only by agreeing to Kashmir joining India rather than Pakistan.

With hostility between India and Pakistan unresolved since a brief war over Kashmir in 1965, no simple solution seems in sight. Today, with two-thirds of the original state in Indian hands and the other third, to the north and west, under Pakistani rule, many Kashmiris have a "plague-on-both-your-houses" attitude, remaining, in spirit if not political fact, resolutely independent.

---

the water and moored in squares by four poles stuck in the lake-bed. On the western shore of Dal Lake, you'll see the white dome and minarets of **Hazratbal Mosque**, famous for its hair of the beard of the prophet Mohammed. Two small squares of land rise out of Dal Lake: Sona-

Carpet merchants use Srinagar bridges as their "shop-windows".

lank, Akbar's Golden Island to the north, and Ruplank, Silver Island to the south.

Two hills, **Hari Parbat** to the north and **Shankaracharya** to the east of town, offer pleasant walks with the reward of a fine view over the lakes and the whole Vale of Kashmir, 134 kilometres long and 40 kilometres wide (82 by 25 mi.).

The famous **Mughal Gardens** are on the eastern shore of Dal

Lake. For the Emperor Jahangir, if the Islamic idea of paradise had a meaning, it was right here, on earth, amid the terraces, pools, waterfalls and fountains, fruit trees and flowers, looking out over the lake with the backdrop of the snow-clad Himalayas.

In summer, there's a sound and light show at Jahangir's personal favourite, the **Shalimar Bagh**, laid out in 1616. Enjoy it as the emperor did, by lingering on each of the four terraces to take in the changing perspectives. The white marble pavilion on the first terrace was for public audiences, the second a private pavilion, the third, in black marble, for the harem, and the fourth reserved for the emperor.

Three kilometres (2 mi.) to the south, **Nishat Bagh**, was laid out in 1633 by Asaf Khan, brother of Jahangir's wife. With 12 terraces, it's the largest of the gardens, lined with fine cedars and cypresses and offering a magnificent view of the lake. Tucked away in a fold of the hills is **Chashma Shahi**, the smallest but in many ways most exquisite of the gardens, drawing its water from a spring running directly down the mountainside.

Excursions from Srinagar

There are several easy day-trips by bus or car from Srinagar into the surrounding mountains. If you're in the mood for a trek on foot, pony or horseback (for which the local tourist information office can advise you on overnight camping facilities with guide and cook), two destinations provide decent accommodation as bases.

The mountain resort of **Pahalgam** is 95 kilometres (60 mi.) east of Srinagar. The route takes you through groves of willow, for the local cricket-bat industry, and fields of saffron. If you wondered why it's so expensive, you need 150,000 of these beautiful purple or white crocuses (only the stigma is orange) for one kilo (2 lbs.) of the stuff that flavours and colours Indian curries and Spanish *paella*—Spain being the only other place than Kashmir where saffron is still extensively grown.

The most popular trek from Pahalgam is 45 kilometres (27 mi.) up to the **Amarnath Cave** (altitude 3,895 m.; 12,742 ft.), sacred to Hindus and so a pilgrimage on festive days for the imposing stalagmite regarded as Shiva's lingam. Only 35 kilometres (22 mi.) from Pahalgam, but much more strenuous is the spectacular **Kolahoi Glacier**.

Gulmarg, 52 kilometres (32 mi.) west of Srinagar and 2,653 metres (8,622 ft.) above sea level, is developing its winter sports in addition to the golf and tennis. Good hiking, too, through the pine forests and meadows carpeted with wild flowers in summer.

THE WEST

The West is, above all, Rajasthan, land of the maharajas, with its desert and lake palaces. But it's also the colourful bustle of Bombay and the ancient splendour of the cave temples of Ajanta and Ellora. With the great bonus, down the coast, of Mediterranean life Indian-style on the beaches of Goa.

Introducing Rajasthan

Rajasthan is one of the most romantic regions in all India. Once known as Rajputana, stretching west from Delhi to the Pakistani Sind and the Punjab, this is where the great Rajput warriors built their desert and mountain redoubts. The splendid palace-fortresses were constructed with granite hewn from the surrounding hills, but also with the dazzling white Makrana marble chosen for Shahjahan's Taj Mahal.

The cities of Jaisalmer and Jodhpur are on the old caravan routes from the Indus Valley through the Thar Desert, for it's a land of cattle-herders, too. Leading their camels, goats and sheep, these noble nomads, with their scarlet turbans and the most ferociously twirlable moustaches you're ever likely to see, are as much a monument of the Rajasthani landscape as the fortresses their forefathers were so often called on to defend.

One of their most spectacular moments is the great annual market-festival at Pushkar in October (see p. 202).

Themselves probably descendants of invading Scythians and Huns, the Rajputs mounted with their fiercely independent spirit, endurance and physical courage the most formidable opposition met by the new waves of invaders—Turks, Afghans or Mughals. The Rajputs' opposition would have been even more formidable if their independent-mindedness had not extended so often to fighting among themselves.

Despite the Rajputs' "foreign" origin, the Brahman priesthood found it wiser to accept their claimed descendancy from the Aryan dynasties of the sun and the moon. They were duly inducted retroactively into the *kshatriya* warrior-caste (a caste to which the Rajputs of the 20th century have continued proudly to adhere, reinforcing their prowess in two world wars and their

Elephants line up like taxis to take visitors around Amber fort.

élite positions in the modern Indian armed forces).

While the neighbouring regions of Malwa and Gujarat came under Moslem rule, Rajputana remained steadfastly Hindu. (Those towns with the suffix -*pur* had Hindu rulers, -*abad* being the Moslem suffix.)

Under the Mughals, some Rajput princes pursued an independent line, though never so far as to threaten the central power. Others, like the Raja of Amber (Jaipur), were happy to send their daughters to the emperor's harem and serve as senior officers in the imperial army. They enjoyed a similarly privileged position during the time of the British Raj.

JAIPUR

When visiting the capital of Rajasthan, it may or may not help,
but at least it gives food for
thought, to know that it was built
according to precise astrological
precepts. Raja Jai Singh II, the
scholar of the stars who dotted
northern India with his collec-
tions of instruments for observing
the heavens, chose an exact date
for moving his capital from
Amber—November 17, 1727—as
particularly auspicious. He proceeded to lay it out according to
the disposition of the most important stars and planets.

But let's begin, as he did, at
Amber, 9 kilometres (5 mi.) north-
east of Jaipur, up on a hill com-
manding a narrow gorge—militarily advantageous but not appropriate for the expanded city
he wanted as his new capital.
The road up to Amber takes
you through classical Rajasthani
landscape, parched hills surrounding Lake Maota where water buffalo snooze in the sun. You
may pass an occasional camel,

time-honoured "ship of the desert" incongruously hauling his load on a cart fitted with the discarded tyres of an aeroplane.

At the approach to the **fortress**, the Rajputs of Jai Singh's Kachwaha clan slowed down their potential enemies—and today's tourist traffic—with a steep elephant-ramp. An elephant with gaily painted trunk and comfortable howdah to sit on will carry you up through the Suraj Pol (Sun Gate) to the **Jaleb Chauk**, a pretty garden-courtyard swarming with langur monkeys and surrounded by the old elephant-stables, some of them converted now to shops.

A staircase zigzags up to the **Temple of Kali**, wife of Shiva, highly ambiguous Hindu goddess of death but also of virginity. Note the silver doors with their *bas-relief* panels depicting the goddess variously riding an ox, donkey, lion or tiger. Her statue was brought from Bengal where the cult of Kali is particularly strong.

The **palace** itself is a relatively subdued example of the maharajas' opulence. Artists banished by Emperor Aurangzeb (see p. 34) found refuge and work in Rajputana, and at Amber their work can be seen in the fluted columns and cusped arches of classical Mughal architecture, as in the gallery around the **Diwan-i-Am** (Hall of Public Audience)—excellent **view** of the surrounding hills.

In the Diwan-i-Khas (Private Audience Chamber), better known as the **Shish Mahal** (Palace of Mirrors), the Rajputs have added their own taste for covering the walls with green, orange and purple glass and the vaulted ceilings with thousands of convex mirrors—strike a match to see the effect.

One of the most inviting places

in the palace is the **Sukh Niwas** (Hall of Pleasure), with its doors of inlaid ivory and sandalwood. Inside, cool water was brought down from the roof through a delicately carved white marble chute and fresh air through the lattice stonework.

The colour of its sandstone has gained for Jaipur the name of "pink city", though it changes colour with the season and time of day from pink to amber to bright orange or dull ochre.

As is appropriate for a descendant of the sun-dynasty, Jai Singh laid out the city on an axis from the **Suraj Pol** (Sun Gate) in the east to the **Chand Pol** (Moon

Ladies watched from Hawa Mahal windows but remained invisible.

Gate) in the west, a main street that is today a lively bazaar.

The town's original central focus was the most elaborate of Jai Singh's **Jantar Mantar** observatories, the final fruit of his labours begun in Delhi (see p. 75). The initiated will appreciate the significance, others just the mysterious atmosphere of the giant cream-coloured gnomons (the solid uprights of sundials) and quadrants and sextants measuring the celestial latitudes and longitudes.

The **Chandra Mahal** (City Palace), directly south of the observatory, has a mystically determined seven storeys and seven courtyards. A palace museum provides an intriguing insight into

Jai Singh's observatories remain a puzzle to modern Indians.

the heyday of the maharajas: their costumes, scimitars and rifles inlaid with silver and jewels, and one rather horrible bludgeon with a double serrated edge.

Overlooking the street is the delightful **Hawa Mahal**, literally the Wind Palace, but actually just a rather grand five-storeyed royal box for the ladies to watch public processions. Its airy projecting oriel-balconies have become the symbolic image of Jaipur. There's a fine view from the top of the zigzag staircase.

JODHPUR

Of all Rajasthan's many fortifications, Jodhpur's **Fort**, perched high on its dauntingly sheer cliffs at the eastern edge of the Thar Desert, must rank among the most imposing.

The Rathor Rajputs built it in the 15th century and were always a belligerent bunch, trouble for both Mughal foes and fellow Rajputs, particularly over at Jaipur. Akbar decided it was better to have them on his side than try to conquer them. Typically, when he married the Maharaja of Jodhpur's sister, Jodh Bai, for whom he built a palace at Fatehpur Sikri (see p. 84–85), there was no question of converting her to Islam.

Outside the fort, as you approach the east gate, you'll see a small domed cenotaph and tombstones marking where sol-

diers fell in defence of the fort against the Maharaja of Jaipur. Cannonball scars on the evidently impregnable ramparts are proudly marked by painted rings. They indicate the vain efforts of the Maharaja of Jaipur, who had hoped to take advantage of a mundane frontier dispute to carry off a promised bride, Princess Krishna Kumari, being held not entirely against her will at the fort. In the end, no one got her—she committed suicide during the battle.

On top of the **ramparts**, the fort displays some of its proudest possessions, some fierce-looking howitzers and cannons, with a fine **view** of the blue and whitewashed city. But behind the

---

What, No Jodhpurs?

Those celebrated tapered riding breeches were in fact the fashion for hunters all over northern India, but it was the Maharaja of Jodhpur who brought them to London, for Queen Victoria's Diamond Jubilee celebrations. Or rather, he didn't bring them, they got lost in a shipwreck and he had to get a London tailor to make him up a new pair. The secret of their peculiar design was out and they became all the rage among English horsemen, along with the dapper maharaja's ankle-length riding-boots, also known as jodhpurs, and his close-fitting Jodhpuri coat.

---

ramparts and the gates, with their sharp iron spikes to stop elephants ramming them, the fortress is much more of a handsome residential palace. This is most notable in the balconies of the **Royal Harem** with their screens of delicately chiselled sandstone latticework.

The palace **museum** has a delightful collection of luxuriously embroidered elephant-howdahs,

babies' cradles and ladies' palanquins (large oriental versions of the sedan-chair). Some of these are entirely closed for the bride to remain invisible, others, for when she's well and truly married, have a little peep hole.

At the **Iron Gate** exit, you'll see on the wall a more poignant side to the life of a maharaja's wife—15 scarlet *sati* handprints of widows who threw themselves onto their husbands' funeral pyres.

In the bustling old city centre of Jodhpur itself, you can't and shouldn't miss **Saddar Market** by the old clock-tower. This is the Rajasthanis' Rajasthan. Under the banyan tree there, any one of a dozen barbers will be happy to give you a shave and haircut or at least a share in the local gossip. In the market proper, the spices and grain are piled in multicoloured mountains, with the merchants chanting as they measure out separate lots of five kilos: "three, three, three", "four, four, four", "five, five, five." And at every corner you turn, the fort looms on the horizon.

Just 8 kilometres (5 mi.) north of Jodhpur, in a pretty park on the site of the old Marwar capital of **Mandor,** is the maharajas' 18th-century mausoleum. Watched over by monkeys, parakeets, crows and pigeons—but also rarer birds for any dedicated ornithologist—are impressive

The Rajputs outdid the Mughals in their taste for riotous colour.

temple-like memorials erected on the site of the maharajas' funeral pyres, along with a brightly painted colonnade of Hindu god-heroes.

If you're heading for Jaisalmer by road rather than rail, it's worth making a short detour to **Osian** to see the dozen or so Hindu and Jain temples, many of them dating back to the 8th century. Somehow the sculpted pantheon of Hindu deities and Jain prophets has survived the elements and Mahmud of Ghazni's iconoclasts.

Back on the road to Jaisalmer, there's one last dramatic splash of colour as you pass fields dotted with mounds of scarlet chilli peppers before you plunge into the desert.

JAISALMER

Situated on the route of the ancient caravans that brought goods from the Middle East and Central Asia, the golden sandstone citadel, protected by a double set of bastions, rises like a mirage from the sands of the Thar Desert.

Jaisalmer was founded by Rajputs of the moon dynasty, the Maharawals, in 1156, making it the oldest of the major fortified cities of Rajasthan. Though much of the modern city—modern in time, not in style—has grown up outside the **fort**, about 3,000 people live within its walls, some of their tiny houses in the narrow side streets dating back to the 12th century. The best view of the citadel is to be had from the terrace of the Jaisal Castle Hotel.

Local artisans have worked the

desert sandstone with the ease of a carpenter chiselling wood. The elaborate sculpture in four 15th-century **Jain temples** within the fort finds its counterpart in the richly carved façades of the **Merchants' Havelis** (mansions) built 200 years later, sheltered from sandstorms on the north-east side of the fortifications.

But more than individual monuments, undeniably handsome but none of them grandiose in the restricted spaces available, it is the general atmosphere of the town, quiet, easy-going, positively timeless, that gives Jaisalmer its special magic. And the whole bathed in the unique light

Women of the desert that surrounds Jaisalmer's fort recall the Arabia of biblical times.

of the desert that adds a shimmer to every stone and a strange liquid translucence to shadow.

To see the **desert** at its best, go out at dawn and perhaps again at sunset. The road beyond Jaisalmer peters out at the village of Sam and the forbidden area of India's military installations on the border with Pakistan. But on the way, there's a "camel-station" where you can take a ride across the sand dunes. (Longer camel-safaris can be organized through Jaisalmer travel agencies.)

Ask the camel-driver to direct you to the uncharted village of **Kuldhara**. Uncharted because it was one of 84 such villages abandoned over 160 years ago by the clan of Paliwal Brahmans who, after living there for centuries, left overnight rather than pay a new, arbitrary land-tax. It still stands, a ghost town of dilapidated square sandstone houses, visited only by the occasional goatherd who may play you a tune on his flute.

Just 9 kilometres (5 mi.) out on the road to Sam, the **Mool Sagar** gardens are popular for picnics in Jaisalmer's blessed but brief rainy season, with pretty little arbours and an old monsoon-pavilion, but it's pleasant all year round.

> ### Titles and Titles
>
> *Rajput princes attached great importance to titles. At first they were known as* Rao, *"chief" of their clan. Akbar made them happy by calling them* Raja, *"King". From there, they promoted themselves to* Maharaja, *"Great King" or, higher-ranking,* Maharana, *then* Maharaja Dhiraj, *"Great King of Kings", and even* Maharaja Dhiraj Raj Rajesur, *something like "Great Hero King of all Kings". You might have thought it would stop there. But no, then came the British, with their "Knight of the Garter", "Knight Commander of the British Empire" and the rest.*
>
> *The princes began to count how many titles they could collect, the all-important thing being the number of initials each comprised. A state crisis might arise if somebody got only a C.V.O. (Companion of the Victorian Order) when his rival was a K.C.V.O. (Knight Companion etc.). The Maharaja of Jaipur, for instance, died happy in 1970 as Lieutenant-General H.H.Maharaja Sir Man Singh Bahadur, G.C.S.I., G.C.I.E.*

UDAIPUR

If Jaisalmer is the city of the desert, Udaipur, in the south of Rajasthan, is its opposite, the city of lakes and gardens. Properly speaking, the lakes are artificial—reservoirs or, just as unpoetically, tanks—created by the Maharana Udai Singh for his new capital by damming up the Berach river after Akbar had sacked his mountain redoubt at Chittorgarh.

The Maharanas of Udaipur, the senior clan of the Rajputs' solar dynasty, had five palaces in and around Udaipur: the City Palace for their winter quarters, the Jagniwas out in the middle of Lake Pichola as a summer palace (better known now as the Lake Palace Hotel), the Jag Mandir, also on Pichola, for celebrating festivals, the Lakshmi Vilas palace for guests beside the second lake, Fateh Sagar, and a monsoon palace up in the Aravalli Hills. It was the white marble of these palaces that Shahjahan

Jaisalmer sandstone balconies are prodigies of intricate carving.

chose for his Taj Mahal after a stay at Udaipur.

Lake Pichola, 4 kilometres (2 mi.) long and 3 kilometres (2 mi.) wide, is the largest of Udaipur's chain of lakes. Cruises are available from the Bhansi Ghat, near the City Palace. This will enable you to go out to the **Lake Palace Hotel**, a monument in its own right, even if you're not staying there. Take a drink at the bar and see the lovely gardens in the interior courtyard. Make for the southern end of Pichola for the best **view** of the whole lake, taking in the two island-palaces and the City Palace beyond.

The 16th-century **City Palace** on the east shore of the lake is now a museum. You'll see the maharana's golden sun symbol emblazoned everywhere, a source of worship during the monsoons. Notice among the displays of weapons and armour a special outfit to disguise horses as elephants. Among the frescoes of festivals and battles, you'll see the story of Princess Krishna's suicide at Jodhpur. It's a sobering thought that the glass baubles as big as golf balls in the mosaics have replaced real rubies and sapphires.

North of the City Palace is the handsome 17th-century **Jagdish Temple**, a rare example of pure Indo-Aryan style untouched by the Moslem influence prevalent at the time, in its own way sym-

bolic of Rajputana's independent spirit. The town's **Folk Museum** has a fine display of traditional Rajasthani art, including puppets, costumes and the whole range of different-coloured turbans worn by the various Rajput clans.

Fateh Sagar Lake can be reached by boat through a canal at the northern end of Pichola, but it also makes a pleasant drive past the gardens of bougainvillea

Perennial water-carrier takes a shower in Udaipur's Lake Pichola.

and lilac of Lakshmi Vilas palace. Stop off to visit the pretty 18th-century **Gardens of Saheliyon-ki-Bari** (Maids of Honour) where the Hindu maharana kept—discreetly away from the centre of town—the Moslem dancing-girls presented him by the Mughal emperor. The gardens are famous for their five fountains which imitate the cherished sounds of the monsoon, from light shower to torrential storm.

Chittorgarh, the fortress and battlefield of the Rajputs' supreme acts of chivalry and sacrifice, makes a good excursion by road or rail from Udaipur. The fort built up on a 150-metre-high (487-ft.) plateau in the Aravalli Hills lies in noble ruin, a beautifully restored relic of three em-

113

battled centuries. You enter on the north-west side and zigzag up through seven splendid gateways, each with built-in guardhouses, to the remains of heroic exploits that have an exalted place in popular legend comparable to those of the

medieval knights of Europe or the samurai of Japan. Stones mark the spots where various Rajput heroes fell defending the fort.

Immediately south of the Main Gate, the 15th-century **Palace of Kumbha**, a Mewar Rajput, is built over the underground cave where Padmini led the first *jauhar* and to which the Rajputs' descendants return every year for a ceremony of commemoration. Notice that

The key to Rajasthan's mystery is the desert, and its faithful guardian is the camel.

some of the walls have been built with pieces of Buddhist temples brought from a nearby village.

Kumbha's 37-metre-high (120-ft.) **Jaya Stambha** or Tower of Victory—the Rajputs did win some, too—was built to celebrate his victory over Sultan Mahmud Khalji of Malwa in 1440. Its nine storeys are decorated with Hindu deities, lions and elephants. But it seems to take its inspiration from the beautifully carved **Kirti Stambha**, a Jain Tower of Fame from the 12th century.

At the southern end of the fort, beside a pond with a little pavilion in the middle, is **Padmini's Palace**, where the tragic princess is said to have passed her last days. It's unlikely that a mirror hanging in the room overlooking the pond is the one in which the sultan got his fatal peek at her, but it helps the guides tell the story.

Do or Die

Rajput warriors placed a horrifyingly high price on their honour. In 1303, Sultan Ala-ud-Din of Delhi laid siege to Chittorgarh, it is said, to win for himself the Princess Padmini, whose beauty he'd been allowed only to glimpse in a mirror. Rather than submit, the Rajputs' wives and daughters committed jauhar, mass self-immolation, while the warriors rode out of the fort in the saffron robes traditionally worn for the last battle unto death.

Over 200 years later came another heroic resistance against the Sultan of Gujarat, ending in another tragic jauhar, in which 13,000 women are said to have died—and 32,000 saffron-clad Rajputs. The last stand came with the devastating attack by Akbar in 1567, and one final suicidal sacrifice and battle.

115

RANAKPUR

Hills and mountains being especially sanctified in the ancient cult of Jainism, you will find in the Aravalli Hills in south-western Rajasthan one of the Jains' most important sanctuaries.

North of Udaipur, a winding mountain road takes you past green terraced fields and mango groves over plunging ravines to the magnificent white marble temple-complex of Ranakpur.

The **Chaumukha Temple**, known as the quadruple temple because of its four central domes, is in fact a complex of 84 domed shrines, each topped by a flag tinkling its bells in the wind.

Built in 1438, the Chaumukha is dedicated to Adinath, first of Jainism's 24 Tirthankaras (teachers) whose truths were revealed by Mahavira (see p. 56–57). As with all the holy places of Jainism, you must remove not only your shoes but all goods made of leather.

Through the entrance hall decorated with sensual sculptures and across the half-moon threshold, you penetrate a positive forest of pillars, symmetrically aligned but each subtly different in its carving.

The richness of the 15th-century temple's materials and the masterful carving of the pillars and domes attest to the prosperity of the Jain merchant who commissioned it. Approaching from the entrance, you'll find him sculpted, on the 2nd row of pillars, 2nd pillar from the left, in a position of prayer facing the statue of Adinath. His architect, Deepa, is also represented, carved with his instruments, in the 3rd row of pillars, 1st pillar on the right. (Restoration work on the temple is carried out by the 14th generation of Deepa's direct descendants.) In one of the main domes, you'll see depicted the elephants hard at work hoisting the roof.

You yourself can climb up to the roof for a fascinating perspective of the flags and domes and their lovely setting of palm, eucalyptus and sacred neem trees surrounded by the Aravalli Hills.

Equally important as a Jain sanctuary, but less accessible than Ranakpur, are the Dilwara Temples on **Mount Abu**, situated in what was a delightful hill-station for the British (and now the Indian bourgeoisie). If you go—and the temples are well worth it—you would do best to take the train from Jaipur or Ahmedabad.

After the arid desert of the plains, the lush green cornfields of the Aravalli Hills are a welcome sight.

AJANTA AND ELLORA

The cave temples hewn from the granite of the Vindhya mountains in the north-west Deccan are one of the great wonders of India.

They are, on any count, masterpieces of technology, since the "caves" are not natural formations, but man-made hollows in solid rock, granite cliffs from which a whole community of architecturally elaborate temples and monasteries has been painstakingly carved with pick-axes, hammers and chisels.

But even beyond the technical *tour de force*, the rock-cut sanctuaries of Ajanta and Ellora comprise superb works of art—sensuous painting and bold, expressive sculpture of the highest order.

Both are within easy reach of the Maharashtra town of Aurangabad. If possible, you should not try to visit both sites on the same day. If you are interested in following the historical evolution of the cave temples, go to Ajanta first, where the oldest caves date back to the 2nd century B.C. Reserve Ellora for an afternoon tour, when its caves, facing west, are illuminated by the sun. At both places, reliable official guides from the office of the Archaeological Survey of India offer their services free of charge.

From the point of view of preservation, **Ajanta** has the advantage over Ellora of having remained untouched for over 1,000 years until British soldiers discovered it during a tiger-hunt in 1819, while Ellora's caves were in constant use (and abuse) as dwelling places.

The use of rock-cut sanctuaries goes back to the time of Emperor Ashoka, in the 3rd century B.C., when itinerant Buddhist monks joined together to form a religious order and the emperor provided them with rock-cut cells as a retreat, *vihara*, during the monsoons. The monks added a hall for communal worship, *chaitya* or temple.

Of Ajanta's 29 caves, all Buddhist, five are *chaitya* temples and the rest, *vihara* monasteries. They are cut from a horseshoe-shaped cliff that stands 75 metres (252 ft.) high above a narrow gorge with a small stream running through it from a waterfall. Originally, each *vihara* had a stairway running down to the stream. (The stone ledge connecting the caves is a modern addition for visitors.)

The caves have been numbered from 1 to 29, west to east. Visiting just nine of them will give you an ample impression of the whole. You should start in the middle, at the oldest caves, then work your way east before returning to the historically later caves at the western entrance.

Cave 10 is probably the oldest of the *chaitya* temples, dated at about 150 B.C. Its nave and aisles are divided by 39 octagonal pillars leading to a *stupa*, the domed focus of veneration, with a narrow apse beyond, permitting the ritual circumambulation. At this early period of Buddhism, there is no representation of the Buddha.

Notice how the excavators, as the cave's creators must be called, have imitated wooden construction in the beams and rafters of the ceiling over the aisles.

Cave 9, is a 1st-century B.C. sanctuary smaller than No. 10 and dominated by the *stupa*. The finely cut two-storey façade with its arched window and Buddha figures in side niches was added much later, probably in the 6th century A.D.

The earliest of Ajanta's monasteries, **Cave 12**, will give you an idea of the monks' sleeping-quarters. If you're not afraid of the pitch-black dark, go in and lie down on one of the two stone beds in the *vihara's* 12 little cells. At each entrance, you'll see holes that held the hinges of a wooden door.

Two kneeling elephants welcome you to **Cave 16**, one of the most important of the later caves created between A.D. 475 and 600. With the Mahayana school of Buddhism now encouraging the worship of a Buddha image, the *stupa* is replaced by a majestic sculpture of Buddha seated in the posture of teaching. As part of the new sensuality, look out for two delightful ceiling sculptures of amorous couples, one distinctly merrier than the other.

With the astonishing richness and vigour of its mural paintings, **Cave 17** represents one of the summits of Ajanta's artistic achievement. Created around the end of the 5th century A.D., the walls are covered with 12 stories of Buddha's adventurous progress towards enlightenment. Buddha's resistance to temptation give the painters a splendid pretext to show the sensual side of court-life as a foil to the Master's spirituality. We see him taming an enraged elephant or, as the warrior Simhala, attacking the Island of Ogresses, while his wife Rani, holding a mirror, languorously prepares her toilet, with hand-maidens holding her cosmetics.

The sculpted Buddha of the shrine is seen with the wheel symbolic of his law and two deer referring to the park at Sarnath where he held his first sermon. On the pedestal, look out for two smaller figures, one of them holding a bowl for alms or offerings —they represent the merchants who financed the cave's construction.

The small *chaitya* of **Cave 19** is notable for the finely carved façade and Buddha statues of its interior, but also the graceful figures relaxing in side niches at the entrance. Visit **Cave 26** for the riot of "architectural" bravura—elaborately ribbed vaulting, carved pillars and a truly Baroque shrine with seated Buddha.

Unlike the rather austere monasteries of the earliest period, **Caves 1 and 2** are richly ornamented. Again there are superb mural paintings of bright-eyed deer, peacocks, monkeys and elephants as well as the opulent palace life which we see Prince Siddhartha riding away from on horseback. But the masterpieces, in Cave I, are two intensely spiritual Boddhisattvas on the back wall on either side of the antechamber.

The caves of **Ellora**, cut out of a whole hillside of basalt rock, are conceived on a much grander scale than Ajanta's. Over the centuries, local villagers have constantly sheltered in them during monsoons or epidemics, so that the wall-paintings have largely disappeared, but the magnificent sculpture has survived.

Starting where Ajanta left off—some of the Buddhist artists may have moved over to Ellora—the 34 caves were created between the 7th and 12th centuries. The first 12 are Buddhist, 17 Hindu, and the other five Jain.

They stretch north-south over 3 kilometres (2 mi.), giving you the possibility of clambering up behind some of them as well as approaching from the cave-entrance, but don't be intimidated—just four or five of the caves will do the trick.

The most important of the Buddhist excavations (1–12) and only *chaitya* sanctuary here, is the 8th-century **Cave 10**. Its rib-vaulted ceiling may remind Europeans of a Romanesque cathedral. The great Buddha seated in the domed stupa is worshipped by eclectic Hindu artisans as Visvakarma, carpenter of the gods, so that the sanctuary is known as the Cave of the Carpenters.

Cave 12 is a three-storey *vihara* dormitory. The sensual female sculptures show the growing Tantric Hindu influence. You must imagine these and the Buddha figures here originally painted in bright colours.

Cut and Paste

As you can see from unfinished caves such as 14 or 24, the sanctuaries were "created downwards", scooped out of the cliff from top to bottom, rather than being built up from floor to roof. Among other differences from conventional architecture—it might be more appropriate to speak of monumental sculpture—roof-beams, columns and arches did not have to serve their usual weight-bearing functions.

The wall paintings are sometimes wrongly described as frescoes, in which paint is applied to a damp plastered surface, whereas here, the technique is that of tempera, paint on a dried surface of plastered cow-dung.

Ajanta cave-painting depicts the sensual life that Buddha left behind him.

Of the Hindu temples (13–29), **Cave 14** is an interesting transition from the Buddhist caves in that, among the pantheon of Hindu gods and goddesses, Vishnu sits in a meditative pose that suggests he may have been sculpturally converted from a Buddha, and two other standing gods are strongly reminiscent of the Bodhisattvas of Ajanta. The sculpture is generally lively: a very dynamic Shiva killing demons and playing dice at his home in the Himalayas; small boys playing with Shiva's sacred bull, Nandi, biting his tail and trying to mount him; in a separate shrine, seven mother goddesses with their children.

The masterpiece of Ellora, indeed one of the major treasures of Indian art, is the astonishing **Kailasa Temple** of Cave 16. With a ground plan the size of the Greek Parthenon and a structure over half as tall again, this was the work of the great 8th-century Deccan king Krishna I. In the process of shaping the temple and its shrines in an area 82 metres (265 ft.) long and 47 metres (150 ft.) wide, leaving the back "wall" of the courtyard 30 metres (97 ft.) high, some 200,000 tons of rock were cut away from the face of the hill.

Whatever was saved in the initial labour of having to haul the masonry needed to "erect" such an edifice was more than counterbalanced by the seven generations of craftsmen needed to complete their amazing carvings *from one piece of rock*. The anonymous

sculptors have presented what seems to be a complete panoply of Hindu tradition—legendary heroes, their battles, the hunt, murder and rape, the weddings of gods and goddesses, and all watched over by powerful elephants and lions.

The result is a classical Hindu temple on the most grandiose scale, which visitors to the south will be able to compare with its undoubted inspiration, the great monolithic temples of Mahabalipuram (see p.189), built just 50 years before Kailasa was begun.

The monumental gateway leads up to the *mandapa* worship hall, with the towering pyramid of the shrine beyond, the whole symbolizing in stone the sacred mythical Mount Meru, Himalayan home of the gods.

After examining the sculpted friezes at courtyard level, get another perspective of the marvellous detail from above on the stone ledge that leads around the top (there's no risk with good shoes and the safety railing).

After Kailasa, the Jain caves (30–34), excavated between the 8th and 13th centuries, inevitably come as an anti-climax, despite their considerable sculptural prowess. **Cave 31** tries to emulate the great Hindu temple on a smaller scale, but the artists were working on much harder rock and had to abandon their effort. The most interesting remains the two-storey **Cave 32**, known as Indra Sabha, notable above all for the upper floor's extravagant carving that is the hallmark of Jain sculptors, and the great elephant, more rigid than Kailasa's, probably because of the tougher stone, but somehow more noble.

A temple built not from the ground up, but hewn from a granite cliff.

BOMBAY

The town's most celebrated monument, the Gateway of India, still describes, for most travellers, its principal function. For those who want to work their way down the west coast to the south before attacking the rest of the country, Bombay remains, as it was for the thousands of servants and soldiers of the British Empire, the natural gateway.

An occasional luxury liner does still glide past the great stone gateway, the famous harbour promenade of the Apollo Bunder and the Yacht Club, once "Royal" and now plain "Bombay", to dock at Ballard Pier. For the rest of us landing at Santa Cruz Airport, the old turmoil of dockside porters and rickshaws that once almost submerged the newcomer is replaced by the equally crazy bustle of businessmen dashing around the country and migrant workers travelling to and from the Gulf.

With skyscrapers shooting up all along the seafront, Bombay is certainly India's busiest industrial and commercial centre—cars, textiles, chemicals, nuclear energy and shipping—and also a major focus for the cinema and the renewal of Indian painting. But the considerable wealth is often juxtaposed with abject poverty, epitomized by sack-cloth hovels on the construction sites, with women carrying bricks on their heads to build luxury apartment blocks.

For anyone not here on business, three days, at most four, should be enough to get a good idea of this huge, exhausting city—with the possible exception of nostalgics of the British Raj (or others fascinated by the phenomenon), who will find a wealth of intriguing relics.

Before starting out on your exploration of the sprawling city stretching in a wide crescent over 20 kilometres (12 mi.) from north to south, go to the very helpful Government of India Tourist Information Office opposite Churchgate Station.

Then begin where King George V did on his momentous visit back in 1911, down on the promontory at the end of Apollo Bunder, a site marked now by the **Gateway of India.** It is one of those monuments that are more moving for their symbolism than their beauty, the exact emotion depending on how you feel about the British Empire it was built to celebrate.

Kipling insisted in his *Ballad of East and West* that "never the twain shall meet", but here the British have done their best by perching four Gujarati domes on this otherwise very Roman concept of a triumphal arch. It was inaugurated in 1924 and the Somerset Light Infantry marched through it to their ships 24 years

Rather than Delhi, Bombay is the place for Raj-buffs to start out, for this was the beginning of the British imperial adventure in India. Once just a chain of swampy, malaria-ridden islands inhabited by a few fishermen and peasants tapping toddy from the palm trees, it didn't seem a great loss to the Sultan of Gujarat when he ceded it to the Portuguese in 1534. They passed it on to the British as part of Catherine of Braganza's dowry to Charles II in 1661. The East India Company picked it up for a song—a rent of £10 a year for the next 62 years.

After years of intimidation by the Portuguese, the Hindu, Parsi and Jewish merchants now flocked into the burgeoning port-city. The island-swamps were dried out and linked together by land-fill to form one Bombay Island, separated from the mainland by the easily bridged Thana Creek. Modern docks were constructed, the first cotton mills in 1853, followed quickly by other factories to instal Bombay's own industrial revolution. The bard of the Raj, Rudyard Kipling, son of the local art school teacher, was born here in 1865. Militarily, Bombay was British India's naval kingpin and, as you will see from the many warships in the harbour, remains today the headquarters of the Indian Navy.

later, the last British troops to leave India.

Facing the gateway is the unequivocally Indian equestrian **statue of Sivaji**, erected in 1961 to honour the Maratha hero of Hindu nationalism who fought against the Mughals (see p.31).

Beside him is the **Taj Mahal Hotel**, a monument in its own right, built by a patriarch of the great Parsi industrialist dynasty, the Tatas. Architecturally another mixture of Western and oriental styles, it is above all a proudly surviving part of the grand old tour that took world travellers from Europe to Shepheard's in Cairo, Raffles in Singapore, the Peninsula in Hong Kong and the Imperial in Tokyo. Even those not staying there get a whiff of the old romance by taking tea in the Sea Lounge for the view of the Gateway and harbour. Is it blasphemous to recall the *ingénue* in the bar who thought the mausoleum at Agra was named after the hotel?

"The Raj District"

Going north-west from the Taj, in the area around the green open space or Maidan that was the heart of British Bombay, connoisseurs will appreciate the architecture that fans call "eclectic" and foes "mongrel".

The old Secretariat might be described as Venetian Gothic,

the University Library French Gothic, the Telegraph Office Romanesque, and the High Court and Cathedral of St. Thomas both, thank goodness, Early English. The architects were British but the artisans Indian, naturally adept at spicing up the design with ornamental detail reminiscent of Rajput forts and Mughal palaces.

On the octagonal spire of the University's 80-metre-high (262-ft.) **Rajabai Clocktower**, built by an Indian benefactor, the national note is emphasized with 24 figures representing the castes of Maharashtra state, of which Bombay is the capital.

In the **Cathedral,** even the most cynical anti-imperialist may be touched by some of the poignant epitaphs for those who died in the military or civil service of their country.

For dedicated Raj-buffs, the supreme example of this Indo-Gothic is the extravagant **Victoria Terminus**, affectionately abbreviated to V.T., once *the* railway station that launched all the adventures into the interior, but now mainly handling Bombay's suburban traffic.

North-west of the V.T. is the bustling **Crawford Market** (even the most hardened Bombay nationalist is not quite accustomed to the post-Independence name of Mahatma Jyotiba Phule). Behind an incorrigibly British redbrick façade, with a couple of nice *bas-relief* friezes by Kipling's father, J. Lockwood Kipling, over the entrance-gate, the stalls of the iron-roofed Crawford still have the original layout of 1865: vegetables to the left and fruit and flowers to the right, fish, mutton and poultry straight ahead.

The Indians' Bombay

Beyond Crawford Market, the area of Bombay that the Indians truly call their own, away from the cosmopolitan Apollo Bunder and the Maidan, inevitably still redolent of their old imperial masters, is known in striking tribute to simple reality as the City.

This is the heart of Bombay's teeming street-life, bringing together Indians from all over the subcontinent to compete with the boisterous Maharashtrans in a dozen different **bazaars**. Among the garishly coloured Hindu temples and simpler mosques of the Moslem neighbourhoods, Jain merchants sell gold in the

Bombay's Dhobi Ghat, the world's biggest open-air laundry.

Zaveri Bazaar, while others deal in silver, brass, copper, leather lace and embroidery. The most notorious market is the Chor (Thieves') Bazaar, where car-owners buy back their own spare-parts and the "Gucci" luggage and "Cartier" watches have never been west of Bombay.

But the Indians' Bombay is also the popular promenade of **Marine Drive**, sweeping in a cres-cent around Back Bay from the skyscrapers of Nariman Point to the smart residential area of Ma-labar Hill, where it's unlikely you'll get to see the Towers of Silence (shown in model form in the Prince of Wales Museum). These are the funeral towers on which Parsis expose their dead to be devoured by vultures.

What you should see, however, before Marine Drive curves round towards Malabar Point, is the permanent carnival of **Chow-patty Beach**. This beach is not for swimming, nor even for sunbath-ing. It's one of the greatest peo-ple-watching spots of western In-dia. Not just for the fakirs and fakers walking on fire, sleeping on nails, climbing ropes in midair or burying their heads in the sand. But for the more sober holy men forming Hindu gods in the sand, the families picnicking and the food-vendors hawking *kulfi* ice cream, *pan* betel-chew and *bhel-puri,* a local fast-food speciality of spicy vegetables.

Museums

The **Prince of Wales Museum**, at the southern end of Mahatma Gandhi Road, is worth a visit for its collection of Rajput and Mu-ghal miniatures and 7th-century sculptures of Vishnu and Shiva from the caves of Elephanta, as well as its fine collection of prehis-toric pottery and stone tools.

The new **Jehangir Art Gallery**, immediately behind the Museum, will give you an opportunity to see the trends in modern Indian art, two of the most important Bombay painters being Tyeb Mehta and Akbar Padamsee.

In Victoria Gardens, home of a sorry-looking zoo, the one animal worth seeing is the great stone elephant brought from Elephanta Island. It belongs to the nearby **Victoria and Albert Museum**, which documents the history of Imperial Bombay.

More up-to-date, the Tourist Information Office can organize a visit, in small groups, to the set of a Bombay **film studio** to watch one of their extravagantly roman-tic productions in progress. (India is the world's most prolific film-maker, far ahead of Hollywood.)

Elephanta

The 7th-century cave-temples of Elephanta Island make a pleasant boat-excursion by harbour ferry from the Apollo Bunder. (On the way, look out for the high-domed nuclear reactors at Trombay.)

Known to the Indians as Gharapuri, Sacred City of the Kings, the island was named Elephanta by Portuguese sailors when they saw the giant stone elephant in front of the main cave (now moved to Bombay's Victoria Gardens). The sailors then proceeded to have musket-practice at the expense of the many magnificent sculptures of Hindu gods in the seven caves. Still, enough survived to make the visit worthwhile.

Carved out of the mountain of rock in the centre of the island, Elephanta's caves may not seem so impressive if you have already visited Ajanta and Ellora (see p. 118), but the main **Great Cave** is an imposing 40 metres (130 ft.) deep and 40 metres wide, divided into aisles by four colonnades. To the west, on a raised platform stands a stone lingam, Shiva's emblem, which draws large crowds on festivals. On the rear wall, facing the north entrance, is the three-headed **Shiva Mahesamurti**, a colossal bust of Shiva as the Supreme Lord. The frontal face of the god has an expression at once powerful and serene, while the angry destroyer, *Bhairava*, looks to the left and his sensuous, almost feminine aspect looks to the right.

Almost as fine, in a panel left of the Mahesamurti bust, is the **Ardhanarishvara**, Shiva as man and woman.

GOA

Time to relax, and this former Portuguese colony is a perfect place to do it. The beaches are superb—all the white sands and whispering palm trees one could wish for. The cuisine makes use of the best seafood in India. And the Goans themselves, of mixed Hindu and Portuguese descent, are a spirited community of people to relax with. Still hanging on are a few glazed-eyed latterday hippies, relic of a bygone age.

As a change from flying down, many people like to take the more leisurely steamer from Bombay (embarkation at the Alexandra Dock). You can book de luxe sleeping-berths for the 22-hour trip to the Goan capital of Panaji (formerly Panjim) and get a good look at the often dramatic mountains of the Western Ghats running parallel to the coast.

After Vasco da Gama had landed down the Malabar Coast

Francis Xavier's Relics

Every ten years—the next time in 1994—the body of St. Francis Xavier is carried from the church of Bom Jesus to be exhibited at the cathedral. But not a lot is left. In 1554 a Portuguese lady bit a toe off, another toe fell off and is kept in a separate crystal box, the right hand was donated to the Catholic community in Nagasaki, while other pieces were sent to Rome.

in 1498, the Portuguese seized Goa from the Sultan of Bijapur in 1510 and held the colony for the next 450 years until Nehru drove them out. Besides being a vital link for Portugal's colonial trade in the Indian Ocean, Goa became, with its succession of Franciscans, Augustinians, Dominicans and Jesuits, together with an Inquisition to hold them in line, a prime base for missionary activity, most notably led by Francis Xavier who came to Goa in 1542. The traders have gone but the missionaries' old churches in Velha Goa still stand and make a fascinating sightseeing trip if you can ever tear yourself away from the beach.

The most popular beaches are **Calangute** and **Dona Paula**, each within easy reach of the capital, Panaji, and excursions out to Velha Goa. If you want to get away from the crowd, the most secluded and unspoiled sands are to be found along the 40-kilometre-long (25-mi.) **Colva Beach**, running immediately south of Dabolim Airport, down to the lovely **Benaulim** and **Betul**.

Velha Goa

The 16th-century churches of Velha (or Old) Goa have been beautifully restored but, without the town buildings that used to surround them, they have a strangely melancholic air of museum-pieces. (The town once had a population of 350,000, with 100 churches.) Today the laterite stone masonry of many of the remaining churches has been covered with lime plaster to protect them against deterioration from the monsoons.

Distinguished by the harmonious simplicity of its rib-vaulted nave, **St. Francis of Assisi** is the oldest church still standing in Velha Goa, perhaps dating back to 1521. The fine arabesque and floral frescoes are the work of local Indian artists who have let themselves go on themes familiar to them, in contrast to their clumsy efforts at portraits of the saints.

The Tuscan Renaissance façade of **Sé Cathedral**, the biggest Christian church in India, has a certain elegance to it despite a loss of symmetry since its north tower collapsed in 1776. The gigantic main altar, dedicated to St. Catherine of Alexandria, depicts in sumptuously gilded panels scenes from the saint's martyrdom.

The granite and sandstone Baroque church of **Bom Jesus** is famous for the silver casket of St. Francis Xavier's relics in the marble mausoleum to the right of the high altar. The mausoleum was designed in Florence, a gift of the Grand Duke of Tuscany.

The Arabian Sea off the coast of Goa, a moment to dream.

THE CENTRE

Here you touch the very soul of India, at the holy city of Varanasi and the Ganga, as well as its sensuality in the temples of Khajuraho. But there's also a reminder of the harsh historic reality of the Indian Mutiny at Lucknow. And you can escape the preoccupations of man at the magnificent wildlife sanctuary of Kanha.

LUCKNOW

As a logical stopover on your way by air to Varanasi (coming from Delhi or from Calcutta), Lucknow is worth a visit for its special place in the history of India's rise to independence. It had been capital of the strategically vital kingdom of Oudh in the centre of the Ganga valley and became a major focus of the Mutiny of 1857 (see p. 38–39).

The old **British Residency** has been preserved as a somewhat ambivalent monument. Initially, it commemorated the stoical resistance of the besieged British community, with the Union Jack kept flying from the abandoned ruin until August 15, 1947. But, since Independence, it is visited more by Indians interested in this relic of their own struggle for self-assertion—and for a family picnic on the lawns.

Located off Neill Road south of the Gomti river, the gutted shell-scarred central building of the Residency stands in beautifully kept grounds. On a lawn surrounded by 24 palm trees, a cenotaph pays tribute to Chief Commissioner Sir Henry Lawrence, who was mortally wounded by a shell on the third day of the mutineers' attack. Nearby, an obelisk honours "Native Officers and Sepoys, who died near this spot nobly performing their duty", for Indians constituted half the 1,600 troops defending the Residency.

A little **museum** inside the surviving building tells some of the history of the siege with a model of the original Residency, some rusty cannons and cannonballs, prints, photos and letters, one of them smuggled in from Brigadier-General Henry Havelock, commander of the relief force: "I can only say hold and do not negotiate, but rather perish, sword in hand."

Down by the river, a short walk north-east of the Residency, is the **Martyrs' Memorial**, inaugurated in 1957 on the centenary of the

Mutiny, to honour the fighters for India's independence.

Lucknow was for centuries a Moslem stronghold and although its community has dwindled since Partition to 30 per cent of the population, it remains one of the two important Indian centres of the Shiite doctrine, the other being Bombay. Its 18th- and 19th-century mosques, however, are without great architectural distinction.

VARANASI

It is probably safe to say that you cannot begin to fathom the mystery of India without a visit to Varanasi*. Not that this ancient city will "explain" all—if anything, its dramatic confrontations of life and death down by the Ganga river, of great scholarship and simple superstition, may only serve to mystify you even further. But the city's ineffable aura of sanctity—comparable to Rome, Mecca or Jerusalem—is for many visitors so overwhelming that it relieves them of any need for rational explanations.

It was perhaps because the Moslem conquerors felt threatened by the very power of the Hindus' reverence for Varanasi that they destroyed it so thoroughly, over and over again. (No

*The name, misheard by the first Europeans as Benares, comes from its position between the Ganga tributaries of Varuna and Asi.

temple in this 3,000-year-old city dates back beyond the 18th century.) And it became a holy city for Moslems, too, Emperor Aurangzeb even trying to rename it Muhammadabad.

The sanctity of Varanasi derives from its privileged situation on the holy Ganga, the life-giving river that Shiva poured down on the plains from his home in the Himalayas. Because of its mythic connection, many Hindus claim Varanasi is the oldest city in the world, but it was probably founded by the Indo-Aryans around 1000 B.C.—old enough.

Established from earliest times as a seat of learning for Hindu theologians, philosophers and poets, it has remained ever since an outstanding centre of the Hindu sciences. It was on the outskirts of Varanasi that Buddha's disciples gathered in the 6th century B.C. to hear his sermon at the Deer Park of Sarnath. Since then, not only Jain monks and Moslems, but Sikhs, too, have proclaimed it a holy city and built monasteries, mosques and temples.

The Ghats

These steep, stone-stepped embankments leading down to the Ganga river are the gathering-places of the pilgrims, more than 250,000 a year. To see the day unfold at the Ghats, you must rise before dawn to join the pilgrims.

The holy men—and women—are up and about, hale and hearty or halt, lame and blind, making their way on foot to the river. "*Ganga Mai ki jai!*"—"Praise be to Mother Ganga!"

Some are *sannyasi,* wandering religious beggars who in old age, having provided for their families, have abandoned their homes, and walked all the way from Madras and further south than that, to stand on these Ghats and pray, to bathe in and drink the waters of the holy river. Or just to sit and meditate this supreme moment of their religious lives.

And the most aged and infirm come here to die, for nothing is more blessed for a devout Hindu

The rising sun on the ghats of the Ganga, the faithful come to pray.

than to die in Varanasi and thus be released from the eternal cycle of rebirth.

All roads in town seem to lead down to the centrally located **Dasaswamedh Ghat**, where Brahma the Creator is believed to have made a ritual sacrifice of 10 horses. At the top of the steps, holy men sit under their bamboo umbrellas, chanting *mantras*, and offering, in exchange for a small coin or a few grains of rice, some sandalwood paste, flowers and water from the Ganga.

At the water's edge, rent a boat and go out to midstream for a view, in the pink haze of sunrise, of the skyline of traditional Hindu temples, south Indian *gopuram* towers, Moslem minarets and Mughal palace domes. In the 5-kilometre (3-mi.) stretch between her Asi and Varuna tribu-

Spots, Sacred and Secular
With the aid of a small mirror
and a graceful arching hand ges-
ture consecrated in temple sculp-
ture all over India, pilgrims use
the white paste to daub a tilak *or*
tika mark on their forehead, a
variety of dots, stripes, triangles,
or crescents, denoting their sect,
according to whether they are
adepts of Vishnu or Shiva.

Women apply a vermilion
parting to denote their married
status. Many women, married or
unmarried, also wear the vermi-
lion spot or tika *(often these days*
in any colour), as a cosmetic
accessory.

---

taries, Mother Ganga describes a crescent, turning north, as the faithful suggest, for one last gesture of farewell to her sacred home in the Himalayas before descending east to the Bay of Bengal. (Ask your boatman to head upstream, towards the Asi Ghat before doubling back as far as the Panchganga.)

Notice how the ritual ablutions, highly elaborate when performed by a learned Brahman, usually just involve a crouching movement at least three times below the water (women bathe in full sari).

But you'll see plenty of less ritual soap and shampoo and, on the stone slabs of the **Dhobi Ghat**, the rhythmic singing, grunt-

ing and thrashing of laundry-washing, too—Mother Ganga is sacred, but also just a river. Out on stone platforms, young men perform gymnastics, part of a self-discipline known as *danda*.

People who might at first be a little reluctant to confront the omnipresence of death along the river will soon be impressed by the simple dignity and serenity of the funeral rites. Families bring their dead for cremation to **Mani-karnika**, holiest of Varanasi ghats.

The body in a white shroud is carried on a bier of bamboo to the river's edge where a few drops of Ganga water are poured into the lips of the dead. The body is then placed on a pyre of perfumed sandalwood set alight by the eldest son or close male relative, who circles the fire five times.

At **Man Mandir Ghat**, you'll spot another of Jai Singh's astronomical observatories. The **Scindia Ghat** is distinguished by its leaning Shiva temple, slowly subsiding into the river. The minarets of Aurangzeb's Alamgir Mosque rise behind the **Panchganga Ghat**, held especially sacred as the mythical confluence of four subterranean tributaries with the Ganga.

The Town

After the ghats you'll be glad to lose yourself for a while in the maze of lanes that form the

Chawk (bazaar), famous for its perfumes and embroidered silks, copper and brassware.

While you're there, look out for the gilded spire and dome of the **Golden Temple of Vishwanath**, the holiest temple of Varanasi but forbidden to non-Hindus. But you can view it from an upper floor of the building opposite, before going behind the temple to the huge Nandi, Shiva's sacred bull, stained vermilion by the libations of its worshippers. Nearby is a mosque in which you can see bits of the Hindu temple Aurangzeb destroyed to build it.

Out at the Varanasi Hindu University, the **Art Museum** has a magnificent collection of 16th-century Mughal miniatures, which many art historians consider superior in quality, if not in number, to the national collection in Delhi.

Sarnath

Now a suburb of Varanasi 10 kilometres (6 mi.) from the centre of town, Sarnath is one of the most hallowed places of Buddhism, the place where Buddha delivered his Deer Park sermon to five disciples, around 530 B.C., the veritable foundation of the religion (see p. 54).

It quickly became, as it still is today, a major pilgrimage site for Buddhists from Japan, China and South-east Asia.

Emperor Ashoka erected the

Not By Faith Alone
It is hard to convince the faithful that the Ganga river is not totally pure. For centuries, those not permitted for religious reasons to be cremated on the ghats—including babies and victims of cholera—have been dropped in the river while people bathe in and drink the water nearby.

Many firmly believe that the Ganga has the power of self-purification, reinforced for some by chemical analyses revealing an 0.05 per cent sulphur content to conquer the bacteria. While religious faith has provided bathers with an undoubtedly strong psychosomatic weapon against contamination, most people living permanently by the Varanasi ghats suffer from gastro-intestinal diseases.

To combat Ganga's pollution of dead bodies, untreated sewage and industrial waste, a $250 million campaign is finally under way. For India's technologically minded government, faith needs a little help.

---

most famous of his edict-pillars here to stand among the monasteries and stupas of which he had ordered thousands built all over the country.

But like Varanasi, Sarnath suffered at the hands of Qutb-ud-Din's troops in 1194. The ruins have been well restored, accompanied by an excellent museum of

Buddhist sculpture that you should save till last.

On the west side of the road from Varanasi, the **Chaukhandi Stupa**, built by a Gupta king in the 5th century A.D., has an incongruous octagonal tower growing out of the top. It was a monument to mark the passage of Emperor Humayun after his defeat in the 1540s.

In a pretty setting of bougainvillea and sacred neem trees, the remains of seven redbrick **monasteries**, dating from the 3rd century B.C. to the 9th century A.D., can be discerned among the ruins.

Since its bricks were carried off to build houses in Varanasi, only a square platform remains of the **Main Shrine** that marked Buddha's dwelling place during his stay at Sarnath.

West of the shrine, surrounded by an iron railing, is the stump and other fragments of **Ashoka's Pillar**, that once stood over 15 metres (48 ft.) high (its sculpted capital is kept in the museum). Notice how the granite's high polish has withstood the elements for over 2,200 years. Its inscription warns, among other things, against dissidence that might upset national unity under his leadership: "No one shall cause division in the Order of Monks."

The dominant feature of the ruins is the 45-metre-high (146-ft.) cylindrical **Dhamekh Stupa**, built around the 5th century A.D. and believed to mark the site of Buddha's sermon. Immediately below eight empty niches (perhaps once holding some of the statues on display at the museum) is a beautifully carved frieze of floral and geometrical patterns interspersed with birds and small seated Buddhas. (This is when a pair of binoculars comes in handy.)

The **Museum** is a treasure-trove of superb early Indian sculpture from the 3rd century B.C. to the 5th century A.D.

Greeting you as you enter is the museum's masterpiece, the **lion-capital** of Ashoka's pillar, a high point of the art of the Mauryan empire. Its power and pride made it an understandable choice as the emblem of India's regained nationhood in 1947. Four vigorous lions, with magnificent manes, stand triumphant back to back atop a frieze of horse, elephant, bull and smaller lion, each separated by a Wheel of Law, resting on an inverted lotus that once connected it to the pillar.

Against the wall, you can see the giant **Wheel of Law** that originally rose vertically above the lions. As a gentle counterpoint, sculpted 700 years later, look out for the lovely **cross-legged Buddha** with its delicately chiselled halo.

(The Deer Park north of the excavations is a modern afterthought, pleasant to relax in, but not related to the original.)

KHAJURAHO

Contemplating a trip to this town, famous for the erotic sculptures of its medieval Hindu temples, many come expecting to snigger. They leave with sighs of admiration. The sandstone temples are marvels of proportion and harmony and the sculptures, ebullient or tender, playful or even occasionally melancholy, have a grace in their uninhibited sensuality that quickly stifles any temptation to smirk.

We have those indefatigable British tiger-hunters to thank once again for uncovering these masterpieces, around 1840, half-buried in earth churned up around them by centuries of monsoons and then overgrown by the jungle. They didn't see the light of day until they were completely excavated in 1923, over 600 years after being abandoned during the Moslem conquests.

Khajuraho was capital of the Rajput kingdom of the Chandellas, a belligerent clan bringing equal vigour to love and war, as is clear from the temples they built from the 10th to the 12th centuries.

The temples are conveniently divided into three groups, western, eastern and southern. The major ones, in the western group, are in a beautifully kept park with well-marked paths leading you easily from one to the other. To see the sculptures at their best, go when the sun is low early in the morning or late afternoon, if possible, both. And go back at night, when the temples are illuminated.

The lovely **Lakshmana** temple dedicated to Vishnu, is one of the earliest, mid-10th century, and the only one to have preserved its four subsidiary shrines at each corner of the raised square platform on which it stands.

Four progressively taller pointed *sikhara* domes rise above the entrance-porch, the *mandapa* hall for worshippers, a larger hall for the temple's dancing-girls, and the inner sanctuary, surrounded by an ambulatory for walking five times round the image of the deity. The majestic silhouette is said to suggest the Himalayan mountain-home of the gods, but this may be more of a hindsight Brahmanic interpretation than the conception of the architect.

The sculptures portray not only the celebrated erotic postures, but also the lively adventures of Krishna, one notably showing him having to use all four arms to subdue a couple of wrestlers.

Visvanartha, built in 1002, is more compact, ultimately more harmonious in its forms than Lakshmana. Among its many delightful sculptures are a fine flute-playing maiden in the interior and, on the south façade, a graceful nymph pulling a thorn from her foot.

KHAJURAHO

The most spectacular temple of the western group is **Kandariya-Mahadeva**, with its three domes culminating in the great 30-metre-high (98-ft.) *sikhara*, composed of row upon row of other smaller *sikharas*, totalling 84 in all.

Created at the height of the Chandellas' power, in the mid-11th century, the sculpture is the most sophisticated and ingenious—*apsara* dancing-girls, *sura-sundari* nymphs, coquettishly yawning, scratching, applying their make-up, playing with pet monkeys, parakeets or with their very cheerful lovers. The Kandariya is the largest of the Khajuraho temples and achieves with its grand scale an added exuberance to the whole life-enhancing spirit of the place. Only the wettest of wet blankets would suggest this was decadent.

The eastern group includes three Jain temples. The most important is the 10th-century **Parsvanatha**, built in the classical Hindu *sikhara*-domed style and incorporating sculptural themes of the Vishnu temples. While the more ascetic religion of the Jains stops short here of any too explicit sexuality, the ambience is clearly contagious and there are a lot of voluptuous full-breasted ladies you don't usually see on a Jain temple.

Khajuraho raises sexual gymnastics to the realm of high art.

KANHA

This will be your greatest chance to see tiger. In fact, from the point of view of the sheer abundance of wildlife, Kanha is probably the best national park in India.

The journey is a little complicated, but well worth the effort. Either fly into Nagpur or, if you're coming from Khajuraho, take a train to Jabalpur, and continue by road. Reserve in advance your accommodation in the forest resthouses.

The best season is from February to May, when you'll see plenty of the beautiful cheetal (spotted deer), blackbuck, sloth bear, gaur or bison (largest of the wild cattle), wild boar, Kanha's unique barasingha ("12-pointer") swamp deer and monkeys galore. The national "Project Tiger" campaign is doing a sterling job here to protect the king of India's jungles, without neglecting the elusive leopard. Bird-watchers should also spot black ibis and the crested serpent-eagle.

Tracking down the tiger is a subtle affair. On your first morning take a jeep-safari at dawn to scout the terrain. The forest of sal trees and bamboo is a sweet-smelling delight, interspersed with rolling green meadows where the deer and gaur graze. Game trackers are out locating the tiger's hunting ground for the evening safari.

Elephants with jungle-wise mahouts set out in mid-afternoon to seek the tiger in the most likely areas, and you follow in a jeep in a combined operation, alert for tell-tale signs: the alarm bark of the deer; a sudden screech of the monkeys; most significant of all, vultures waiting for the tiger to abandon the left-overs of what he's caught. When the elephant has located a tiger, the mahout signals and you hop aboard his howdah to penetrate the jungle. *Et voilà!*

SANCHI

Just a short drive (45 km.; 28 mi.) from Bhopal, the ancient stupas of Sanchi with their magnificently carved gates and stone railings are, together with the caves of Ajanta (see p. 118), the most admired Buddhist monuments in India. The sculpture also provides a fascinating insight into daily life of the 2nd and 1st centuries B.C.

The site, a 91-metre-high (300-ft.) hill on the Vindhya plateau, dates back to the 3rd century B.C., when Emperor Ashoka, organizing Buddhism as a national religion, ordered stupas containing the Buddha's relics to be built all over the country.

Stupas were originally earthen burial mounds. Buddhism developed them as shrines of plaster-covered brick or stone, in which was embedded a casket containing relics of Buddha or his disciples. Crowned by a stone *chhattra* (umbrella) symbolizing majesty, the stupa was usually built on a raised terrace with a wooden fence (later replaced by stone railings) to enclose the path for the circumambulation of the shrine.

Like so much of India's ancient architecture, the stupas of Sanchi lay concealed in the jungle until uncovered by the British in 1818, this time with unfortunate results. Delay in their proper excavation and restoration nearly a century later led to most of the stupas being plundered by treasure-hunters and villagers needing masonry for their houses.

Luckily, what survives is still superb: three stupas and some interesting remains of temples and monasteries from the 5th to the 12th century A.D.

The **Great Stupa**, also designated as Stupa I, built in the late 1st century B.C., envelops a smaller mound erected nearly 200 years earlier by Ashoka. It is surrounded by two stone railings, a square one on the terrace and a second enclosing a circular paved ambulatory up on the stupa itself, reached by a double staircase.

In the terrace railing are four great *torana* gates, deliberately set just off the north-south and east-west axes, perhaps to deceive evil spirits. They are formed by square posts with sculptured panels, topped by three architraves (crossbars) one above the other with groups of dwarfs, elephants or lions.

At this early period of the religion, Buddha himself is nowhere represented in human form, but you'll see him symbolized by the horse on which he rode away from the worldly riches of his palace, the wheel of law, his footprints or the pipal tree under which he found enlightenment.

The rest of humanity is abundantly present in his worshippers, his adversaries, graceful dancers and nubile *yaksi* tree-nymphs. Despite the asceticism preached by Buddhism at this time, it's clear that the ivory-carvers and carpenters brought in to apply their skills to the sandstone were given free rein for their joyous sensuality.

The smaller **Stupa III**, northeast of the Great Stupa, has only one *torana* gate. It was originally built to contain the relics of the two principal disciples of Buddha, preserved in a casket with fragments of bone and small jewels. The flat-topped mound of **Stupa II** is down on the western slope of the hill. Its circular balustrade with four L-shaped entrances has much simpler decoration, flowers, animals and Buddha-symbols. Historians note that the horsemen are using stirrups, the earliest known example of their use in India.

THE EAST

This region encompasses the birthplace of Buddhism at Bodh Gaya, the great Hindu temples of Bhubaneshwar, and the tremendous challenge of Calcutta, an amazing confrontation of vitality and hardship. You can cool off amid the green, green tea-plantations of Darjeeling or on a trek in the mountains of Sikkim.

CALCUTTA

The town's reputation for the squalor of its slums has so deeply imbedded itself in the world's imagination that it comes as a delightful surprise to discover the Calcuttans themselves to be the liveliest bunch of people in the country. Much more than its monuments of stone, India's treasure is its people and nowhere is this more true than Calcutta.

Bengalis are quite simply irrepressible, and the challenge of just coping with daily life in this clogged-up city of 10 millions has strengthened their resilience and sharpened their wit so that an alert and curious visitor cannot fail to be fascinated and even in the end, yes, entertained.

Survival here has become a creative art and it is surely no accident that Calcutta remains India's intellectual and cultural capital long after relinquishing the business of government to Delhi. It was the home of writer Rabindranath Tagore, India's first Nobel Prize winner, as well as philosophers Ramakrishna and Vivekananda. Poets, painters, musicians, dancers, actors and journalists still make their national name here.

After the rather stodgy establishment-minded press of Delhi, you'll find Calcutta's newspapers bright, ebullient and downright vitriolic. If Bombay's film-makers are masters of melodrama, Calcutta's cinema is known for its sensitivity and poetry, producing faithful mirrors of village and city life in the hands of such directors as Satyajit Ray and Mrinal Sen. It is the proper home for the country's best museum, simply and aptly the Indian Museum.

For all their ardent nationalism, Calcuttans retain a strong, if sometimes sardonic attachment to things British, particularly the language which you'll find spoken here with the most British of accents and often considerably more elegance than the British themselves can muster.

The West Bank

Even if you're not coming into Calcutta by train, start your visit over at **Howrah Station**. The crowds in and around the station will give you something of a baptism by fire, and you'll soon realize only a small fraction of them are actually there to take a train. For many, the station is a home, its entrance-hall and platforms a dormitory—and kitchen.

After the Howrah show, you'll welcome a rest at the charming **Botanical Gardens**. Laid out in the 18th century, they boast over 35,000 species of flowers and shrubs. It was here that the first tea cuttings were brought from China to found the plantations of Darjeeling (see p. 155) and Assam.

The gardens' pride and joy is the enormous 200-year-old banyan tree, a native son known to botanists as *Ficus bengalensis* or strangling fig tree. Some fungus disease destroyed its central trunk, but it still thrives with a circumference of 400 metres (1,300 ft.), thanks to the pillar-like aerial roots that it puts down to support the ever-spreading branches.

The **Howrah Bridge** takes you across the river to the city centre but is in itself a major national monument. The spectacle is astonishing. Connoisseurs insist this massive steel suspension bridge habitually stages the world's most magnificent traffic jams. It is a great place to gauge the Bengali temperament and very satisfying to be the only person there without an urgent need to get somewhere.

The City

The centre of the city is another park, the **Maidan**, but this one was landscaped for strategic rather than recreational reasons, to give a clear line of fire on all sides from **Fort William**, rebuilt by Robert Clive on a more defensible site than its predecessor.

Like Britain's Hyde Park, the Maidan attracts ferocious soapbox orators predicting the end of the world, but also some wonderful charlatan peddlers of patent medicines, suspicious-looking smoking weed and equally dodgy tea and snacks.

In the north-east corner, **Ochterlony Monument**, named after some obscure British warrior and one of many Calcutta landmarks taking a long time to get used to its new name (in this case, Shahid Minar), is the focus of the city's very boisterous political rallies.

Over by the river is **Eden Gardens**, with pond and Burmese pagoda, and the venerable Calcutta cricket grounds.

At the southern end of the Maidan is the most British of all monuments in Calcutta, perhaps in the whole country, the huge domed **Victoria Memorial**, a museum of the great queen's

145

Toehold on the Hooghly

When the body of Shiva's wife, Kali, was chopped up after her death, the little toe of her right foot fell on the bank of the Hooghly river and that's where the village of Kalikata grew up. Together with the villages of Sutanuti and Govindpur it was sold to the East India Company in the 1690s to establish the trading counter of Calcutta.

It was the Nawab of Bengal's attack on the British settlement in 1756 that brought Robert Clive's crushing reprisal at Plassey and the consolidation of the British Empire in India. Calcutta, with its port-connection to east Asia and subsequent development of jute, cotton, silk and tea, was its capital for the next 150 years. But Bengalis in general and Calcuttans in particular were trouble-makers, violently stirred by the growing nationalism. The British found it prudent to move the political capital to Delhi in 1911.

Since Independence, when Partition cut Calcutta's jute and other industries off from their natural hinterland in eastern Bengal, the city has had its economic difficulties compounded by a huge influx of refugees from what is now Bangladesh. The town remains a hotbed of radical politics, stronghold of the Indian Communist Party.

reign, indeed a veritable history of the Raj. Anglo-Renaissance in style, with a touch of the Mughals, its white marble came from the same Rajasthani quarries as the Taj Mahal's. It was commissioned by Viceroy Lord Curzon and paid for by "voluntary contribution" of the maharajas and nawabs.

You can catch up on the latest in Indian avant-garde art—and meet some of the more Bohemian citizens of Calcutta—at the **Academy of Fine Arts** on the south-east corner of the Maidan.

Running along the eastern edge of the Maidan, **Chowringhee Road** (officially renamed Nehru Road) marks the old European neighbourhood whose mansions once won Calcutta the rather wishful name of "City of Palaces". Now, Chowringhee is the town's busiest shopping street, with hotels and cinemas, gigantic film billboards featuring actresses in wet saris, and a roadway so chock-a-block with pedestrians, cows, rickshaws and bicycles that cars are very often seen going backwards.

At the corner of Chowringhee and Sudder Street, the **Indian Museum** provides an excellent home for art treasures from the ancient Maurya and Gupta eras that had been disintegrating after centuries of exposure to the merciless natural elements. Thus, in its **Bharhut Gallery**, it has preserved the great Buddhist carvings on the stone railings from the Bharhut stupa (2nd century B.C.) in central India, comparable to the stupa carvings of Sanchi (see p.142). The **Gandhara Room** has the earliest Indian sculptures representing Buddha in human form (1st century A.D.), though, coming from a region of Greek settlements (today part of Afghanistan), these Buddhas make him look more like a Greek philosopher than an Indian sage.

In **Dalhousie Square** (also called BBD Bagh), on the site of the original Fort William north of the Maidan, was once the throbbing centre of Britain's imperial bureaucracy. Here, scribblers of the East India Company—*babus* to friend and foe—duplicated and triplicated everything they could lay their hands on, in the augustly-named Writers' Buildings. (It now serves just the Government of West Bengal, but with an apparently undiminished number of *babus*.)

It takes a sleuth to find the original site of the **Black Hole**, at the big domed General Post Office on the west side of Dalhousie Square, since most Indians aren't interested in helping you. They regard the incident (see p.36) as an exaggerated piece of British propaganda to justify Clive's military retaliation. A plaque marks the spot in an arch on the northeast corner of the post office.

Most major British Indian buildings prior to the 20th century were built not by an architect but by a soldier-engineer copying existing plans from back home. The imposing **Raj Bhavan** (Governor's Residence) north of the Maidan, copied Kedleston Hall in Derbyshire, and the nearby **St. John's Church**, Calcutta's first cathedral, is a version of London's St.-Martin-in-the-Fields. Look in the south aisle for John Zoffany's bemusing painting of *The Last Supper* which uses East India Company men as models, with the painter's sworn enemy, Mr. Paull, as Judas. In the church cemetery is the tomb of Job Charnock, the Company official who founded Calcutta.

A bizarre tribute to Western art and architecture is to be found at the **Marble Palace** of the wealthy landowning family of Raja Majendra Mullick Bahadur, in the tiny Muktaram Babu Street northeast of Dalhousie Square. This Palladian villa turned museum, with a park and menagerie of exotic birds, recalls William Randolph Hearst's Castle in California in its crazy juxtaposition of ancient Roman and Chinese sculpture, Venetian chandeliers and Sèvres porcelain, Flemish masters and naughty French erotica. And the odd Mullick still hanging around to play Chopin in the ballroom or billiards in the parlour.

149

BHUBANESHWAR

As you fly down the coast from Calcutta, you'll suddenly spot a veritable small forest of tall domes in a town with a lake at its centre. These are the temples of Bhubaneshwar, one of the most important of India's holy cities.

The capital of Orissa is also a centre for easy day-trips to the ancient Jain cave-monasteries of Udaigiri, the amazing chariot-temple of Konarak and sacred pilgrimage town of Puri—with beach.

Once there were literally thousands of Hindu and Jain sanctuaries in and around Bhubaneshwar. Some 500 can still be traced, most of them in ruins, but 30 are in visitable form. Three or four are masterpieces of Hindu architecture.

The oldest of the temples (7th and 8th centuries), rather "squat" compared with the full flower of Bhubaneshwar's architecture, are grouped around the sacred "Ocean Drop" lake of **Bindu Sagar**, the focus for bathing and purification ceremonies before the annual festivals.

East of the Bindu Sagar is the 10th-century **Muktesvara**, an ex-

quisite rust-coloured sandstone temple dedicated to Shiva, with its own small bathing tank and gracefully arched *torana* gate at the entrance. There is great peace and dignity in the temple's perfect proportions. The low curved pyramid on the hall of worship and elegantly ribbed elongated *sikhara* dome over the sanctum present the classic silhouette of Orissa temples.

Like their sisters in Europe, the gypsies of India make wonderful use of jewellery.

The 11th-century **Rajarani**, standing on a platform at the end of a pleasant garden, is a more robust structure than the Muktesvara, with a more pronounced pyramid over the worship-hall and powerful *sikhara* behind it.

The greatest of the city's temples is the **Lingaraja**, late 11th century, south of the Bindu Sagar. Off limits to non-Hindus, it can be viewed from an observation platform (specially erected for the purpose by Lord Curzon). You'll find binoculars particularly useful here to appreciate the splendid detail of the carving on the soaring central tower that dominates what is a whole complex of temples. It is dedicated to the Lord of the Three Worlds, Tribhuvanesvara, from which Bhubaneshwar takes its name.

Udaigiri

The ancient Jain cave-monasteries of Udaigiri are close to Bhubaneshwar airport and you may find it convenient to visit them before the Bhubaneshwar temples.

Excavated from a solid sandstone hill in the 3rd and 2nd centuries B.C., the Udaigiri (Sunrise Hill) caves provided dwellings for priests and monks at a time when Jainism was the state religion in the kingdom of Kalinga.

Steps cut in the rock take you right of the main entrance to the two-storeyed **Rani's Monastery** (Cave 1), decorated with carvings of elephants, maidens praying and court dancers. Unlike the caves of Ajanta and Ellora (see p.118), there are no temples or central halls for worship.

Further up the hill, **Ganesha Gumpha** (Cave 10) is set back on an esplanade and guarded by two sturdy stone elephants on the porch holding branches of mangoes. The friezes are more sophisticated and show archers riding elephants and a king of Kalinga reclining with his queen. Cave 14, **Hathi Gumpha** (Elephant Cave), is important for the long inscription above the entrance detailing King Kharavela's conquests and irrigation projects during his 13-year reign around 50 B.C.

Konarak

The **Sun Temple** of Konarak is the most formidable of ruins, conceived as nothing less than a gigantic stone chariot for the great sun-god Surya cantering inland from the Indian Ocean.

The *sikhara* that once towered 60 metres (200 ft.) into the air, like some symbolic divine charioteer, has gone, but the grandiose pyramid of the **Jagmohan** (Hall of Audience), where the priests officiated, still soars above 12 pairs of huge stone wheels sculpted into its platform and drawn by seven galloping horses.

The temple was built in the 13th century, probably by the Orissa king Narasimha celebrating his successful resistance of the Moslem invaders. The *sikhara* toppled, its porous stone not only victim of coastal storms and plunderers, but also of the over-ambitious conception of its builder. As you climb over the remains of this triumphant monument, you'll find it has a decidedly secular air.

Surya was given his due with dignified green chlorite statues of *parsva-devatas* (sun-deities) in niches facing the four points of the compass, but the emphasis of

The sun-god's giant stone temple chariot has ground to a halt.

much of the sculpture profusely decorating the walls is on the life of the king—his battles, the royal hunt and life at court. The sensuality of the aristocratic lovers recalls Khajuraho (see p.139).

The wheels themselves, symbols of the Hindu cycle of rebirth, have beautifully carved spokes and hubs decorated with kings and gods. Beneath the wheels are lively friezes of elephants playing with children. Look out, too, for a giraffe, indicating the Indian west coast's early contact with Africa.

Masterpieces among the free-standing statuary are the war-horses trampling the king's enemies and splendid elephants crushing the demons.

European sailors, for whom the temple was an important landmark to keep out of the shallows of the Orissa coast, called it the Black Pagoda—to distinguish it from the "White Pagoda" of Puri's whitewashed Jaggannath Temple down the coast—and nearly had it turned into a lighthouse. After the *sikhara* tower had collapsed, the British saved the pyramidal Jagmohan by pouring concrete into its core, and now the Archaeological Survey of India are heroically performing massive restoration work on the sculpture.

> ### Wheel of Life
>
> *Jaggannath, as the Universal Lord, an incarnation of Vishnu the Preserver, offers Hindus of all castes the opportunity to escape the torment of perpetual rebirth. And so hundreds of thousands of pilgrims converge on Puri all year round, but most of all for the June festival when the three great wooden chariots of Jaggannath and his brother and sister are drawn through the streets. Then, the faithful can liberate themselves by touching the crudely carved wooden deities (models of which are sold in the town).*
>
> *Although orthodox followers of Vishnu insist Jaggannath is a positive, life-giving force, the belief persists that the frenzied intensity of the festival has led some to seek ultimate release by hurling themselves under the huge wheels of the Jaggannath chariot, whence the English word "juggernaut", meaning any great force demanding utter self-sacrifice.*

Puri

Even if you can't be in Puri for the tremendous Rath Yatra Festival in June, the town is worth a visit to see the phenomenon of a community devoted almost entirely to the "industry" of its great **Temple of Jaggannath**, either directly or by trading with the pilgrims.

Non-Hindus are not permitted within the temple precincts, but you get a good **view** from the roof of the Raghunandan Library close to the temple wall. Some 6,000 priests, artisans and other workers are employed in the temple grounds. Of the four main buildings, whitewashed and decorated with garishly painted sculptures, the first is where worshippers bring their offerings of flowers and fruit, the second for sacred dances, the third for viewing the divine effigies, which are enshrined in the sanctum of the fourth and tallest edifice.

Puri also has a beautiful **beach**, south-west of town, ideal for cooling off. Those aren't sandcastles the Indians are making, they're miniature temples. This is the *Swarga Dwara*, Heaven's Gateway, where the faithful wash away their sins.

DARJEELING

Before you overdose on temples or just the heat of the plains, follow the example of the long gone British of Calcutta and get up into the hills and greenery leading to the celebrated tea gardens of Darjeeling.

At 2,185 metres (7,100 ft.), you catch your breath in the more rarefied air and take in the splendours of the Himalayas—Kanchenjunga over in Sikkim (see p. 160) and, if you're lucky on a clear day in April and May or late September and October, Mount Everest itself, up in Nepal.

In 1835, the raja of the then independent kingdom of Sikkim was pressured into ceding Darjeeling to the British. They had spotted it as a healthy place for their soldiers and East India Company employees to recover from the ills of the plains, but above all as strategically useful for controlling a pass into much-contested Nepal. With the tea plants from seeds smuggled out of China and an influx of plantation labour from Nepal, the little village of 100 souls grew by 1849 to a community of 10,000.

Permits for Darjeeling and Sikkim

Being close to the militarily sensitive border-areas of Chinese Tibet, Darjeeling and Sikkim require permits (free). Darjeeling is easy: either you obtain it automatically at the Indian Embassy back home when you get your visa or, if you're flying up to Bagdogra, the closest airport, your passport will be stamped right there. You'll need a special permit for trekking beyond Darjeeling, but it's no trouble.

A permit for Sikkim, which is extendable for a limited period, should be requested, via an Indian Embassy, at least four weeks before you leave home and collected at the Deputy Commissioner's Office in Darjeeling. (Theoretically, the permits are also issued at the Ministry of Home Affairs in Delhi, but the red tape is awful.)

Today, Darjeeling is part of West Bengal, but Nepali remains the official language and most people are physically of Nepalese and Tibetan origin. Buddhists account for 18 per cent of the population.

A major part of the pleasure of Darjeeling is the journey. Although you're driving along narrow mountain-roads, you'll feel much safer than in the plains because everyone takes infinitely more care, lorry and bus drivers clearly subdued by the ravines.

But the best way to travel up—at least part of the way if you're too impatient to take 6 hours for the whole 80 kilometres (50 mi.)—is by the **Darjeeling Himalayan Railway**, more popularly known as the "Toy Train", which starts out at Siliguri, not far from Bagdogra. Built back in 1881, the tiny steam-train on its 60-centimetre (2-ft.) track climbs, loops and zigzags through dense forests of sal, Chinese cedar and teak, alive with jungle birds and mountain streams.

Look out for Pagla Jhora, the Mad Torrent, just after Gayabari Station, Gladstone's Rock, shaped like the old statesman's head, near Mahanadi Station, and, at Kurseong, your first good view of Kanchenjunga, 8,586 metres (28,168 ft.) high, the world's third highest peak, (after Mount Everest and Pakistan's K2).

The railway-builders admitted it might have been safer to dig tunnels, but they preferred to go "round the mountain" to give you a better view of the terraced tea gardens and the valleys plunging down to the Bengal plains. Certainly, when you reach the railway's highest point, 2,257 metres (7,407 ft.) at **Ghoom**, the view as you hover out on the loop over Darjeeling is in every sense breathtaking.

The only relics of the British Raj are the now all-Indian and still very private Darjeeling Club (though a planter might sneak you in) and a couple of tea-rooms and Edwardian hotels like the Windermere (coal-burning fires and hot water bottles at night).

The real British legacy is in the **tea gardens**, now all Indian-run, which provide a beautiful green setting for the town and a fascinating insight into the growing

India shares its tallest mountain, Kanchenjunga, with Nepal.

and processing of tea before it gets to your pot (see p. 209). Among those open to visitors, without any obligation to buy, are Makaibari and Happy Valley. (Your hotel will help you make an appointment.)

There's a popular excursion to drive by jeep to **Tiger Hill** before

dawn. Indians and Westerners go for different reasons, though both with an almost religious excitement as the night fades. From an observation platform, you can get a terrific view, away to the north, of Kanchenjunga and, on a good day, just a small jagged peak in the distance—yes, Mount Everest. But you'll notice the Indians are facing east. What matters is not the rare opportunity of seeing the world's tallest mountain, but the *sunrise*.

For a closer look at the true roof of the world, consider a seven-day camping trek, on foot or on pony, up to **Sandakhpu** (3,650 metres, 11,700 ft.). You'll get better views of Kanchenjunga and Mount Everest, but above all, you pass through lovely forests of rhododendron, chestnut, magnolia, and, in April and May, the orchids are in bloom.

Armchair mountaineers can visit the excellent museum at Darjeeling's **Himalayan Mountaineering Institute**. It has some fascinating memorabilia of Himalayan expeditions, in particular the equipment used by local boy Sherpa Tensing Norgay, here Indianized as Shri Tensingh, when, with Edmund Hillary, he was the first to conquer Everest in 1953.

Preparing a winter wardrobe in the ancient kingdom of Sikkim.

SIKKIM

Once again, a great part of the joy is the journey itself, by road up to the capital, **Gangtok** (1,768 m.; 5,800 ft.) in eastern Sikkim through some of the most spectacular scenery in India, with rivers roaring through narrow rocky gorges, steep green valleys whose every contour is outlined by terraced rice paddies, and hills covered with dense forest and rich vegetation.

To protect India's border with China and put an end to the unrest over the raja's autocratic rule, Sikkim, after many years of semi-independence, was incorporated into the Indian Union in 1975. The people of Sikkim are in a large majority Nepalese, together with Lepchas, the country's original settlers known also as Rongpan, people of the ravines, and Bhutias from Tibet.

The colourful Tibetan Buddhist monasteries are one of the attractive sights in the valleys around Gangtok, the most easily accessible being **Rumtek**, built in 1968 after China's seizure of Tibet drove the maroon-robed monks of the Karmapa sect into exile.

Other older monasteries, from the 18th century, at **Pemayangtse** and **Tashiding**, some 150 kilometres (92 mi.) west of Gangtok, are well worth visiting, but access may be restricted at times by the military authorities.

PATNA

The capital of Bihar serves as a useful base for visiting the important Buddhist sanctuaries of Bodh Gaya, Rajgir and Nalanda, but its bustling bazaars, first-class sculpture museum, a major Sikh temple and the spectacular views of the Ganga river make Patna itself worth at least a day of your time.

Patna is one of India's most ancient cities, already in existence 2,500 years ago, when Buddha and his Jain counterpart, Mahavira, were active in the region. Known then as Pataliputra, it became the capital of the Mauryan emperors, most notably Ashoka in the 3rd century B.C., when it was one of the largest cities in the world, nearly 3 kilometres (2 mi.) wide and stretching some 12 kilometres (7 mi.) along the Ganga.

In the 19th century, the British used Patna as one of their two opium manufacturing and distributing centres—the other being at Ghazipur in Bengal—to keep China supplied with its favourite drug. The old opium warehouses can still be seen down by the river in Gulzarbagh district, now used by the Government Printing Press.

But one of the city's more bizarre yet impressive edifices, the **Golghar** on the west side of town near the river, is evidence of the more altruistic side of British activity in Patna. This great flat-topped dome, a granary 27 metres (87 ft.) high, was erected in 1786 by Captain John Garstin, as an inscription says on the outside wall, "for the perpetual prevention of famine" in the district (following the great famine of 1770). The interior makes a perfect whispering gallery. Climb the 148 steps that wind up around the dome to the top for a fine **view** across the town and the Ganga river.

The granary lies on the edge of the **Maidan,** a large open ground where Mahatma Gandhi used to hold mass prayer-meetings.

Go and stand in the middle of the new **Ganga Bridge** to catch for a moment a sense of the immense place that the river has in the lives of the Indians. The Ganga is nearly 3 kilometres (2 mi.) wide at this point in its journey to the Bay of Bengal. In the dry season, you can watch people working on the edge in vast fields that will disappear as the river rises in the monsoons.

Since you may be unable to visit the Sikhs' Golden Temple at Amritsar, their **Har Mandir Takht** in old Patna, east of the modern city, will give you a chance to see this unique community in one of its four holiest sanctuaries. The white marble temple is built on the birthplace of the last of the gurus, Govind Singh (1666–1708), who called on the Sikhs, in the face of repeated persecution, to be prepared to defend their faith by armed force (see p. 54). The well that served Govind Singh's house still works, now a marble shrine.

The sanctuary exemplifies the religion's combination of piety and militancy. With a gentle fervour, a priest will explain the higher principles of the faith and show you, among the guru's relics in the main shrine, his cradle and shoes, but also his dagger, sword and four steel arrows. Upstairs above the sanctuary, priests and neophytes chant together from the holy scriptures of the *Adi Granth* in a hall that is also a museum of the guru's life, Punjabi history and, as an admonition to the young, the tortures suffered by Sikhs at the hands of the Mughals.

Spare some time for the **bazaar** near the temple—attractive bamboo and sturdy leather goods, both cheap.

Patna Museum has a remarkable collection of Mauryan sculpture, the most famous being its 3rd-century B.C. polished stone *yaksi* (symbol of fertility), a nubile maiden wielding a yak's tail fly-whisk. Two other magnificent pieces are the elegant, even sensuous Buddha figures of the 9th century, a four-armed *Padmapani*, bronze inlaid with silver, and a reclining *Avalokitesvara* of gilt bronze.

Bodh Gaya

The site of the pipal tree or *bodhi*, tree of wisdom, under which Gautama Siddhartha became the Enlightened One, Buddha, constitutes one of the four great pilgrimages associated with his life.*

A couple of hours train or car ride south of Patna, the sanctuary is on the outskirts of the town of Gaya.

E.M. Forster fans might like to pay their own pilgrimage, about 25 kilometres (15 mi.) north of Gaya, to the dark foreboding Barabar Caves which provided the setting for the "Marabar incident" in his novel *Passage to India*. But, as Forster himself noted, the caves have no special artistic merit. Still, it makes a nice picnic.

The towering **Mahabodhi Temple**, dating back at least to the 6th century, evokes the *gopuram* temple gateways of southern India. In keeping with early Buddhist tenets, there is no figurative representation of the Buddha on the outside, but there is a large gilded statue from a later period inside. Behind the temple, you'll find the spreading branches and multiple trunks of the sacred **Bodhi Tree**, believed to have grown from a sapling of the one that stood here 2,500 years ago. Pilgrims drape its

*The other sites: of his birth at Lumbini (Nepal); of his first sermon at Sarnath (see p. 137); of his death at Kushinagar, north of Varanasi.

branches with white and saffron veils.

A stone platform with lotuses carved on its base marks the Buddha's seat. Two giant footprints symbolize his presence and stone lotus bowls mark the steps he took after his enlightenment,

The spice of a million curries, near Nalanda's ancient university.

when wondering whether to spread the message. Walk across to the pool where Buddha bathed before beginning his meditation and where today, among the lotus leaves, Hindus and Buddhists follow his example.

The little **museum** has some fine stone stupa-railings from the 1st century B.C., comparable in form to Sanchi's, but much simpler in their carving. The blackened

granite Buddhas are from the 9th and 10th centuries.

The international importance of the Bodh Gaya pilgrimage can be seen in the Japanese, Thai, Tibetan, Burmese and Chinese temples surrounding the sanctuary. They offer a useful opportunity to compare the various national styles of religious architecture.

Waiting for Nirvana

The demons did not make it easy for Gautama Siddhartha to achieve his enlightenment. As he sat there beneath the pipal tree, for 49 days, the demons played the age-old game of "bad guy, good guy" to get him to crack. First, they hit him with whirlwind, tempest, flood and earthquake. He just sat there. Then the devil Mara brought in his lovely daughters, Desire, Pleasure and Passion, to seduce him with song, dance and caresses. He just sat there. They offered to make him king of the world. He just sat there until they gave up and went away.

Buddha's ordeal was a godsend for Indian art. In the early centuries of Buddhism, when it was considered sacrilegious to portray the Buddha in human form, his torments and temptations provided sculptors with a rich alternative source for their creative imagination.

Rajgir

This ancient city (north-east of Bodh Gaya on the road to Nalanda) has been holy both to Buddhists and Jains since the 6th century B.C. As Rajagriha, capital of the Magadha kingdom, it was frequented at different times by Buddha and his contemporary Vardhamana Mahavira, founder of the Jain religion.

The surrounding hills are topped by temples of both religions, the best known being on **Gridhakuta** (Vulture's Peak) where Buddha is said to have converted the Mauryan warrior-king Bimbisara to his doctrine of non-violence.

The Japanese have built a great white **stupa** on Rajgir's principle hill, which you can reach by aerial ropeway, a pleasant means of surveying the rugged countryside.

Nalanda

To get the most out of the fascinating ruins of the great monastery and university of Nalanda, we recommend you use the services of a guide from the local offices of the Archaeological Survey of India.

In the 3rd century B.C., Ashoka founded the first monastery in this suburb of Rajagriha (Rajgir), which became a great centre of learning under the Gupta kings some 600 years later. By the time the Chinese sage,

Hiuen Tsang, visited Nalanda in the 7th century, it was a celebrated and thriving university, teaching philosophy, logic, history, grammar and medicine, as well as Buddhist theology. It sent missionaries to spread Buddhism to Tibet and attracted scholars from China, Burma, Thailand and Cambodia. It was destroyed by the Moslems at the end of the 12th century and the monks fled to Nepal and Tibet.

The **museum** has a good model of the original university and monastery buildings, worth studying before you go out to the site. It also has a fine collection of bronzes from the 9th to the 12th centuries.

On the **excavation site**, you will see remains of dormitories, the refectory, kitchens, baths, lecture halls, libraries and temples.

Try Cambridge, It's Easier

According to Hiuen Tsang, Nalanda University had 1,500 teachers and 10,000 students, all on scholarships funded by Nalanda's "endowment" of 100 surrounding villages. But getting in was not a piece of cake.

Entrance examinations were exactly that—you couldn't get past the entrance to the university before answering a tough oral question on philosophy, posed by the gate-keeper. Only ten per cent got through the gate.

THE SOUTH

Travelling between Delhi, Bombay and Calcutta, it's very easy to forget that southern India exists at all. The attitude towards it of northern Indians tends to be rather disparaging, not unlike that of many American northerners towards their southern states. But a tour of the peninsula quickly reveals a bright and cheerful people, more relaxed than most northerners, with a culture as rich and varied as their greener landscapes—and beautiful beaches on the Malabar and Coromandel coasts.

The darker Dravidians that make up most of the southern populations don't mind being considered different from northerners, but they don't want to be disregarded.

For one, they were among India's earliest settlers. Archaeologists trace their origins to the builders of India's first cities, Harappa and Mohenjodaro up in the Indus valley. Their religion

165

already included fundamental elements of Hinduism such as Shiva's phallic lingam and his sacred bull, Nandi, *before* the Brahmanic Indo-Aryans arrived on the scene.

Driven south, the Dravidians remained not only geographically separate, but also politically independent, impervious to the successive waves of foreign invaders.

Hindu bastions against the Moslems until the late 16th century, they were most of the time by no means united. The Hoysalas of what is now Karnataka, the Cheras of Kerala, the Cholas, Pandyas and Pallavas of Tamil Nadu, all fought among themselves until the kingdom of Vijayanagar (Hampi in modern Karnataka) emerged as the dominant force in the 14th century.

But each of these kingdoms showed great cultural vitality, even exporting their temple-builders, along with their spices and ivory, to Burma, Malaya, Cambodia and Java. Suffering less than the north from the ravages of Moslem iconoclasts, their temples have survived in profusion and in much better condition.

Karnataka's granite hills— like the stone walls of some forgotten giant's garden.

166

Bangalore is in the vanguard of India's modernization, and Madras, without the same knack for self-promotion as Bombay, quietly produces twice as many feature films, while Madurai and Thanjavur (Tanjore), Belur and Halebid remain custodians of the peninsula's ancient art treasures. The strong regional identity of the south has repeatedly foiled attempts to spread the Hindi language through the south as the national language. On the east coast they point out that Tamil literature is much richer than Hindi. On the west, the people of Kerala (speaking Malayalam) boast the highest literacy rate in the country.[*]

Much better served by the rains, with some parts benefitting from the peninsula's two monsoons, in the summer and early winter, the south's vegetation is luxuriant and colourful. There are coconut groves on the Malabar west coast, palmyra palms on the Coromandel east, and in between, a more arid landscape of rugged mountains and dramatic rock outcroppings, relieved by a sudden flare of "Flame of the Forest" trees, hibiscus or deep green jungle, plentiful streams, lotus-ponds and lakes with scarlet lilies.

---

[*]70% for the whole state, compared with 61% for the next highest, the district of Delhi, and the national average of just over 36%.

BANGALORE

Modern and efficient, with good communications, the capital of Karnataka (formerly the state of Mysore) makes a convenient and comfortable gateway to the western half of the peninsula.

Under the British Raj, Bangalore, at an altitude of 930 metres (3,000 ft.), had been the summer refuge for its Madras-based officials. Their taste for parks and greenery, thriving in the pleasant climate, had made Bangalore the "garden city". The spectacular growth of India's industrial boom town in electronics, aviation, telecommunications and machine tools has noticeably changed the climate since the 1970s, several degrees hotter than in the old days as the concrete gained ground on the greenery.

But there are still pleasant walks to be had in **Cubbon Park** and the terraced botanical gardens of **Lal Bagh**.

The Bangalore-Mysore road makes a delightful introduction to the green and pleasant land of the south, along tributary streams of the Cauvery river, past groves of mango trees, sugar-cane fields and rice paddies, suddenly broken by a soaring mountain of solid granite, which director David Lean made the location for the fateful picnic in his film of *Passage to India*. If you want, you can visit Srirangapatnam and Somnathpur (p. 171) on the way.

MYSORE

The home-town of the fabled maharajas regains a flicker of its old glory every October with the great Dussehra festival, when the heir of the former rulers of Mysore state is paraded through the streets on his golden throne surrounded by gorgeously caparisoned elephants (see p. 202).

But even if you can't make it for the festival, Mysore remains a pleasant, airy city, famous for its manufacture of incense—sandalwood and frangipani, jasmine and musk, creating an urban aroma markedly different from the prevailing scent of burnt cowdung in northern towns.

If the maharaja no longer runs the place, his enormous **palace** is very much there, lit up at night by thousands of light-bulbs, by day a museum showing off his riches. The present building was constructed only in 1897 (after its predecessor burned down, apparently because the maharaja was tired of it and wanted a new one) and represents all the excesses of Mughal nostalgia and undigested Victoriana. Great doors of solid silver open onto a multicoloured décor of marble, mahogany and ivory. The highlight is the palace **art gallery** with its oil paintings of the maharajas striking very British landed-gentry poses and a glass case with, as the label puts it, a "rolled gold replica of the British crown", set between

---

Diamonds Will Do It

If the great Mughal emperors turned to the ladies of their harems more for political intrigue and court ceremonial than for sexual adventures, the Maharajas of Mysore did not have the same priorities. One of them learned from a Chinese scholar that powdered diamonds made an ideal aphrodisiac. The aging but eager prince promptly crushed practically all his kingdom's stock of sparklers, but the ladies were not impressed. He did begin to have more success when his favourite, horrified by this destruction of what, after all, are a girl's best friend, persuaded him to let her personally prepare the powdered potion.

---

a brass tea-kettle (bigger) and coffee-pot (smaller).

Up on the steep **Chamundi Hill**, south-east of the city centre, one of the maharaja's guest houses, Rajendra Vilas, has been converted into a hotel—excellent for tea on the terrace with a splendid view of Mysore. On your way back down, take a look at the massive black **Nandi** bull, Shiva's sacred mascot, with chains and bells, real and sculpted, hung around its neck.

Among popular attractions are the Mughal-style **Brindavan Gardens**, 19 kilometres (12 mi.) north of Mysore, worth visiting at night when the fountains are floodlit.

Srirangapatnam

The names of many southern towns are almost longer than their main streets. About 12 kilometres (7 mi.) east of Mysore, Srirangapatnam is important as the site of hard-fought battles against the Moslem ruler Tipu Sultan in the 1790s, by which the British clinched their control of the peninsula.

The fort taken by Lord Cornwallis and one Colonel Arthur Wellesley (later famous as the Iron Duke with the rubber boots) no longer stands, but the sultan's elegant little summer palace, **Darya Daulat Bagh**, has been preserved as a museum honouring the courageous resistance of Tipu and his swashbuckling father, Haidar Ali. There's a pleasant garden to stretch your legs.

Somnathpur

Somnathpur's **Kesava Temple**, built in 1268, is one of the jewels of south Indian architecture.

The star-shaped structure is small, scarcely more than 10 metres (30 ft.) high, its three *vimanas* (shrines) standing on a low platform, but achieves a positive grandeur in miniature, enclosed in its courtyard completely isolated from the rest of the village.

Plenty of apples each day to keep the Bangalore doctors away.

Epic Extraordinary

To understand the place in Indian culture of the Mahabharata, you must imagine the Bible combined with Homer's Iliad. With more than 90,000 stanzas, it's the world's longest poem, 15 times longer than the Bible. Besides grandiose tales of courage and treachery, romance and cunning, it also includes sacred texts such as Krishna's great sermon known as the Bhagavad Gita.

Here, with sacrilegious brevity, is the story: King Dhritarashtra is forced by blindness to give up his throne. He offers it to the Pandavas, five sons of his brother Pandu. But his own sons, the Kauravas, want the kingdom for themselves and drive out the Pandavas. When Dhritarashtra seeks to reconcile the feuding claimants by dividing the kingdom between them, his sons trick the Pandavas out of their share with a game of dice and force the Pandavas into exile for 13 years.

More treachery ends with a bloody war involving all the kings of India and quite a few Greeks, Bactrians and Chinese, too. The righteous Pandavas emerge victorious, rule for many years in peace and glory, then renounce their throne to go on a holy pilgrimage to the Himalayas, where they enter the City of the Gods. After 90,000 stanzas, they deserve the rest.

The temple is dedicated to Vishnu, in his various aspects: as Janardana, the awe-inspiring punisher, portrayed by a rigid, solemn-looking statue on the north *vimana*; as Kesava, the Radiant, after whom the temple is named but whose statue is missing from the central shrine; and as Venugopala, the friendly, flute-playing Krishna on the south shrine, with another little Krishna as cowherd listening pensively at his feet.

Although it has a domed *sikhara* on each shrine, the temple's overall effect remains "horizontal" in the classical style of the Hoysala kingdom, emphasized by the layers of narrow parallel carved friezes running around the walls. Not a square centimetre of the temple's surface is left unsculpted. An unusual feature in the Hoysala temples is that their carvings are signed by the sculptors.

Like the statuary of Romanesque and Gothic cathedrals portraying events from the Bible, these carvings are intended to be read like a book by those who had no access to the scriptures, reserved for the Brahmans. They tell the stories of the gods, of the mischievous tricks of Krishna, as a child stealing butter from his mother and as a young man stealing saris from girls bathing in the river, and of the great adventures of the epic *Mahabharata*.

BELUR AND HALEBID

The most comfortable way to see these two important Hoysala temples is to visit them on either side of an overnight stay at Hassan, 120 kilometres (75 mi.) northwest of Mysore.

Belur's **Chenna Kesava Temple** is dedicated, like Somnathpur's, to Vishnu the Radiant, but was built 150 years earlier, in 1117. (Beware of the local legend that the Belur, Halebid and Somnathpur temples were all designed by the same architect).

The Belur temple's flattened silhouette gives it an unfinished look, but it's by no means certain that towers or domes were ever planned. As at Somnathpur, it is the exuberant profusion of sculpture covering the walls rather than the overall form that gives the temple its impact.

The friezes of musicians, drummers, dancers and animals bring the building to life, once again recounting the legends of the gods—Shiva the demon-killer—or scenes from the *Mahabharata*—ace archer Prince Arjuna shooting a fish while looking the other way. But the masterpieces are the larger bracket fig-

The sunflowers blare out a brassy chorus in the fields of Halebid.

ures: a beautiful huntress, girls dancing or singing, another about to spray her lover with rose-water. The detail is astounding. By the south doorway, on a vine chiselled beside the head of a girl dancing with a demon, you can find a lizard hunting a fly.

Halebid's **Hoysalesvara Temple**, 16 kilometres (10 mi.) from Belur, dedicated to Shiva and his wife Parvati, is the biggest of the Hoysala temples but suffered from Moslem iconoclasts so that it's worth visiting the nearby **museum**, too, where some of the best of its statues are now kept. The astonishingly intricate carving of the bracket figures in the temple dancing-hall is achieved by working with relatively soft steatite soapstone, which the open air subsequently hardens like granite.

SRAVANABELAGOLA

Fifty kilometres (30 mi.) east of Hassan, on the Bangalore road, you come to Vindhyagiri Hill rising some 140 metres (463 ft.) above the plateau with, on its top, one of the most dramatic monuments in all India, the statue of **Gommatesvara**. To get to it, you must climb barefoot—the hill is holy ground—up 644 steps cut in the rock. Take it easy and you'll find it well worth while.

Erected in A.D. 983, the statue crowns a sanctuary established in the village of Sravanabelagola 1,400 years earlier by the Digambara ("space-clad") sect of Jains who regarded total nakedness as part of the abnegation necessary to achieve enlightenment (see p.57). In the 4th century B.C., Chandragupta, founder of the Mauryan dynasty, is said to have converted to Jainism at Sravanabelagola and fasted to death. (The priests now officiating are Svetambaras, dressed in white.)

Coming upon the statue at the top of the hill, even though you may have already seen it from a distance and don't find its clumsy proportions stunningly beautiful, is an awe-inspiring experience.

This Jain saint looms 17.5 metres (57 ft.) tall, carved from a granite monolith polished white by centuries of libations with milk. Gommatesvara, son of the prophet Adinath, is completely naked except for a vine-creeper winding itself around his legs and arms. The creeper symbolizes the impassiveness he is said to have observed in this upright position of *pratimayoga* which he adopted for one whole year in response to his brother's lust for worldly power. An anthill and serpents at his feet symbolize the mental agony that the faint smile on his lips shows him to have conquered.

COCHIN

One of the most charming towns in the country, where Christians, Jews, Moslems and Hindus live in much greater harmony than they seem to manage elsewhere, Cochin makes a delightful gateway to the Malabar coast and the relaxed life of Kerala.

On a narrow peninsula separated from the mainland by lagoons and small islands, the old part of town is known as **Fort Cochin**, where Vasco da Gama set up Portugal's first Indian trading station. He died there in 1524 and was buried in the **Church of St. Francis**, the only Portuguese building still standing, subsequently converted by the Dutch to a Protestant church. The great navigator's remains were returned to Portugal in 1538 but his tombstone can still be seen on the

The saintly Gommatesvara resists nature's creeping irritations.

Keeping the Faith on the Malabar

The first Jews arrived from Palestine on the Malabar coast, at nearby Cranganur, in the early centuries of the Christian era. Far from their Roman persecutors, they traded peacefully with Hindus or with Arab merchants from the Persian Gulf.

In time, their community was reinforced by new refugees from Babylon and Persia and then by others expelled from Spain and Portugal in 1492, spreading out along the coast.

But as luck would have it, the Portuguese settled there, too, bringing their Inquisition and stirring up the hitherto friendly Moslems. The Jews moved together to Cochin, under the protection of the local Hindu raja. The Portuguese came down from Goa to smash the synagogue in 1662, but it was restored two years later. Today, as the community fades away, there's another problem: no kosher butcher left in Cochin, but, they say, what's wrong with vegetarian?

---

south side of the church, set in the floor surrounded by a brass rail.

At the water's edge, on this northern tip of the peninsula, you can see in action the fishermen's beautiful **Chinese dipping nets**, a system imported from the China seas whereby the nets are slung over a pyramid of four poles, lowered into the water and hoisted out again by a system of rock-weights and pullies.

The **Jewish quarter**, referred to by street-signs as "Jew Town", is in the district of Mattancheri immediately south of the fort. In the narrow streets of spice-merchants and tailors, the Star of David, *menorah* candelabra and Jewish names are more plentiful than the Jews themselves. At Indian Inde-

Hand-drawn Cochin rickshaw, vestige of a vanished colonial era.

pendence there were perhaps a couple of thousand, but the next year, the state of Israel was founded and massive emigration has left only a few dozen here and in the neighbouring town of Ernakulam. The **Synagogue**, with its crimson tabernacle and blue Chinese tiling, was built in 1568—the oldest in the British Commonwealth, as the Beadle will tell you. He'll also show you the Copper Plates granting land-rights to a Jewish community on the Malabar coast back in A.D. 379.

Get away from all thoughts of city life with a **backwaters trip** through the coastal lagoons and canals and around the fishermen's island-villages. The local Government of India Tourist Information Office can help you

hire a motor-boat with a two-man crew, at least for a half-day, but you may never want to return to dry land.

You'll see fishermen working their own dipping-nets in front of their huts or flinging hand-nets out with the whirling motion of an Olympic hammer-thrower. On another island, beside colourful gardens where women clean their shrimp at the water's edge, you can see the ecumenical peace of a church surrounded by palm trees, with a Hindu temple on one side and a mosque on the other. From time to time, you may be accompanied by a whole flotilla of dugouts poled along by children. On the way back, stop off at **Bolghatty Island** in the Cochin lagoon to take tea in the pleasantly faded elegance of the Dutch governor's 18th-century mansion (transformed into a hotel).

Wildlife enthusiasts may want to visit the nature reserve at **Periyar**, a very pretty 194-kilometre (120 mi.) drive from Cochin, where you can watch wild elephant, gaur (bison) and a multitude of birds, from the unique vantage point of its artificial lake. Look out for the elephant herds swimming across the lake, trunks raised like snorkels. Plan on two or three days, as anything less is likely to be a waste of time.

KOVALAM

The big town is **Trivandrum**, with an international airport (mostly for migrant workers going to and from the Gulf), but the only real reason for foreigners to go there is that it's 15 kilometres (9 miles) from the best **beaches** in India. Coconut palms, papaya, bananas, white sand and surf (but beware of the strong currents)

make Kovalam the ultimate in happy-go-lucky *dolce far niente*. Not a temple, not a museum, not a palace in sight. Enjoy.

For people who are visiting Kashmir and want to notch up a trip to the other end, India's southernmost point is **Cape Comorin** (two hours by road from Kovalam), meeting-point of the Arabian Sea and Indian Ocean. Nice thought to look out there and think there's nothing between you and Antarctica. It's usually a very noisy tourist trap, but you might like to see the ocean's wonderful colours when a full moon rises from it at the same time that the sun is setting.

Page 178–179: Cochin inherited its dipping-nets from trade contacts with China. Below: No curried duck, strictly for export.

MADURAI

The ancient capital of the Pandya kings and one of the world's oldest cities, Madurai has always been an important repository of Tamil culture and is today a bustling university town, Tamil Nadu's second largest after Madras.

The feverish religious activity swarming around the 11 towering gopurams of the **Great Temple**, 17th century in its present form, gives you a most impressive sense of the intensity of Dravidian Hinduism.

Its **Minakshi Devi Shrine** is dedicated to a pre-Hindu "fish-eyed goddess" incorporated into the Hindu pantheon along with her husband, Shiva, whose **Sundaresvara Shrine** stands next to it. The grand Madurai festivals in April and May celebrate their marriage, symbolically reconciling the Dravidians with the Indo-Aryan invaders.

Enter the temple-precincts at the main eastern *gopuram* and walk round to the Minakshi shrine to the south. Since, as usual, the interior of the shrines is off-limits to non-Hindus, get a good view of the whole temple and the shrines' glistening golden roofs by climbing, somewhat hazardously up the last narrow

Madurai's shrine to the fish-eyed goddess Minakshi is part of a veritable temple-city.

and slippery flights of stairs, to the top of the **south gopuram**.

Back at ground level, visit the arcaded **Golden Lotus Tank**, the temple's ritual bathing place. At the west end of the tank is a detailed scale model of the whole temple complex.

The busiest area is the **Kambattadi Mandapa**, the ambulatory leading to the Sundaresvara (Lord of Beauty) shrine. Worshippers in slow procession prostrate themselves, bringing offerings of coconut and fruit, and toss tiny balls of butter onto two blackened statues of Shiva. In the north-east corner is the **Hall of 1000 Pillars** (in fact, 997) with finely carved bizarre lion-elephants, and the heroes of the *Mahabharata*, the virtuous Pandava brothers from whom the Madurai Pandyas claim descent.

Outside the east wall of the temple is the **Pudhu Mandapa**, Hall of Audience of the 17th-century king, Tirumalai Nayak, who built the temple. It's now a bustling bazaar of tailors, metal-workers and other artisans.

Stop off at **Tirumalai's Palace**, about a kilometre south-east of the Great Temple. You'll find an elegant relic of former splendour, with cusped arches and massive pillars modelled on the great Rajput palaces of Rajasthan, but also unmistakeably tubby Dravidian gods on a frieze running around the courtyard.

TRICHY

This is one colonial name, an abbreviation of the equally European Trichinopoly, that is stubbornly resisting the general trend to Indianization, the official name being Tiruchchirapalli, City of the Sacred Rock.

Today, its principal importance is as a base for visiting Tamil Nadu's great temple-complexes of Srirangam, Thanjavur and Madurai. But every schoolboy, at least of the old school, knew Trichy for the British defeats of the French there in the 1750s to gain control of the south.

The famed **Rock Fort** that was the main focus of these battles looms over the city atop the great 83-metre (270-ft.) solid granite hill which gave the town its name. From early days the almost impregnable Rock served as a sanctuary, graced by temples and cave-shrines. Steep steps lead up to the Hall of a Thousand Pillars, the shrine of Shiva and the Temple of Ganesh, from which there is a fine view over the Cauvery river, the towers of Srirangam and the rugged plains beyond. Look out on the way up for the 7th-century stout-pillared Pallava cave-shrines.

The French have maintained their presence in Trichy with the Jesuit College of St. Joseph and the adjoining red and buff neo-Gothic church of Our Lady of Lourdes.

Srirangam

The temple precincts of **Sri Ranganathaswami** (on an island formed by two arms of the Cauvery river, just a couple of kilometres from Trichy) enclose a complete township of shops, booths and dwelling houses, with a population of some 60,000. Beyond the outside wall are the temple's farmland, coconut plantations and a large square lotus-covered bathing tank.

The temple itself, dedicated to Vishnu and already a thriving theological centre by the 11th century, was founded at least a couple of thousand years ago—tradition takes it back to the Flood. Its present form of seven concentric rectangular walled courts, culminating in an inner sanctum, dates from the 15th and 16th centuries, after it was liberated from Moslem invaders who had used it as a fortress, but many of the sanctuaries are much older.

You enter on the south side, through an elaborately ornamented *gopuram* gate-tower characteristic of south Indian architecture. Pass under a series of these soaring *gopurams* from one courtyard to the next to witness religion as a full-time daily occupation. The streets are crammed with vendors selling shrine-offerings of sweets, curds, coconut, flower garlands and holy images. Elsewhere, men are cleaning the stables for the temple elephants and storehouses for the chariot-shrines that carry the deities through the streets during the festivals. Notice the handsome pillared verandahs of the dwelling-houses.

Non-Hindus are allowed as far as the fourth courtyard. Here, on the south side, look for the shrine of **Venugopala Krishnan**, with its charmingly sculpted figures in the famous Hoysala style of the temples at Belur and Halebid—notice the girl with the parakeet, important in Indian literature as the go-between bearing messages for lovers.

Climb up to the terrace overlooking this shrine for an excellent **view** over the *gopurams* beyond the fourth courtyard to the golden *vimana,* inner sanctum, and its arched roof with god Vishnu portrayed on each side (binoculars especially useful here).

Most spectacular of all, in the eastern courtyard of the fourth enclosure, is the **Sesharyar** worship-hall with eight carved pillars of magnificent rearing horses and their proud warriors. The boundless energy of these minutely de-

That's not water in those pots, but potent fermented palm-toddy.

tailed 16th-century sculptures honouring the military prowess of the great Vijayanagar kingdom is a summit of south Indian art.

Thanjavur

Known to the British as Tanjore, this was the historic capital of the great Chola kingdom which spread Tamil culture to Burma, China and South-east Asia, where its sculpture and architecture can be seen to this day in the temples of Cambodia, Thailand and Java.

Commercial enterprise, military power and religious fervour went hand in hand. Almost more than the divinity of Shiva, the massive 11th-century **Temple of Brihadisvara** celebrates the victory of the Chola kingdom over the Pallavas of Kanchipuram and the Cheras of Kerala. It set the style for the monumental Dravidian temples.

The accent is on the grandiose: the temple's principal *vimana* shrine is a 13-tiered pyramid 66 metres (222 ft.) high. Shiva's sacred bull, Nandi, is on a similarly colossal scale, as is the phallic lingam, believed to be the biggest in India. Frescoes depict in gory detail the head-chopping necessary to achieve victory. But a more graceful touch is provided by the panels of Shiva demonstrating the 108 basic poses of sacred dance—*bharata natyam* (see p. 199).

MADRAS

Of India's four great metropolises, Madras is far and away the most easy-going and pleasant to get around. Heading for a population of 5 million, it's nonetheless remarkably uncrowded. The people are unstressed and affable.

There's no town in India where southern Californians or Mediterraneans would feel more at home. The beach, my friends, is 12 kilometres (7 mi.) long. If you've been on the road a long time, this is the place to get your business done—banking, mailing

---

Ivy League Connection

Among the many memorials to British military heroes in St. Mary's, Americans may be pleased to see a plaque honouring the subsequent founder of one of its great universities, Elihu Yale, a former governor of the Fort. But Yaleys have nothing much to be proud of here. The British merchant was fired in 1692 after five years as governor for making a large and dubious private fortune while in the service of the East India Company. New England clergyman Cotton Mather, himself a Harvard man, got Yale to part with some of his ill-gotten gains to endow a new college to be named after him if he was the biggest donor. Elihu sent a parcel of goods that sold for £562, but nobody did better.

---

packages, picking up letters from home at the *poste restante* counter of the General Post office.

Madras was set up in 1642 as the British East India Company's first east coast trading station, principally for the shipment of cotton and sugar. After the defeat of the French in the 1750s, it took a grateful back seat in Indian affairs, far from the turmoils of northern India. These days, fiercely independent-minded Tamil politics make the place more lively at election time, but less heated than, say, Calcutta, Bombay or the Punjab.

Fort St. George is now the home of Tamil Nadu's state government and the Indian

Madras's memory of its Victorian age is more serene than that of other big Indian towns.

Navy—you can see what the British Royal Navy used to do here in an interesting little **Military Museum**. (Because of Madras's role as a naval base, the harbour is out of bounds.) The most interesting British "relic" inside the Fort is **St. Mary's Church**, a Wren-like structure dating back to 1680.

One of the most picturesque streets in the old town, across the railway tracks north of the Fort (an area once known, as was often the custom in colonial days, as Black Town) is **Armenian Street**. Still the centre of a small Armenian community, there's a busy street-market and, in a cool, tree-shaded garden, an open-air colonnaded church.

The **State Museum**, on Pantheon Road, possesses some excellent Buddhist bronzes as well as a comprehensive collection of Dravidian sculpture and architecture. From the 9th-century Pallavas and Cholas to the increasingly elaborate style of the Vijayanagar kingdom (1336–1565), the statues and architectural models make a fascinating demonstration in stone of the glory and power of south India.

The two main arteries of the city are the busy shopping centre along Mount Road and the broad and airy Beach Avenue, where you'll find the University, Madras Cricket Club and, at the southern end, **San Thomé Cathedral**. This simple, even austere, neo-Gothic Catholic church houses what is claimed to be the tomb of St. Thomas.

> ### Doubting Thomas
>
> *When Jesus was fixing the disciples' assignments to spread the Good Word around the world, Thomas was apparently given India.*
>
> *"Whithersoever thou wilt, Lord, send me," said Thomas (according to the Apocryphal Acts of the Apostles), "but to India, I will not go."*
>
> *Then Gondophernes, a Pahlava king on the north-west frontier, sent for a master carpenter to help with the building of a new city. Thomas's professional pride overcame his hesitant evangelistic fervour and he realized it was an offer he couldn't refuse.*
>
> *He converted Gondophernes and continued proselytizing through the south to the Coromandel coast, where he is said to have suffered martyrdom, speared to death while praying in a cave (in the south-west corner of modern Madras).*

Mahabalipuram

The ancient port of the Pallava kings, a high point in any tour of south Indian monuments, is only 60 kilometres (36 mi.) south of Madras, but we recommend you, if possible, to stay there overnight (rather than make a day-trip from

Madras). It has good hotel accommodation on the beach, enabling you to see the famous cliff-carvings, *ratha* shrines and Shore Temple down by the sea both in the early morning and at night—with luck, by moonlight.

Known originally as Mamallapuram, the town was named after King Narasimha Mamalla (630–668), "the great wrestler", in whose reign the extraordinary temples and shrines were begun.

Like the cave-temples of Ellora (see p.120), most of the monuments are carved, rather than built, from solid rock, in this case the last cliffs and boulders of the vast granite plateau that ends at the Coromandel coast.

South of the village is a group of **Rathas**, five free-standing monolithic shrines hewn from one continuous table of rock. Imitating elements of the region's wooden and brick-construction, some of them have the same arched or domed roofs as the inner *vimana* sanctuaries to be seen at Srirangam or Thanjavur (see p.187), for which these may well have been the models.

The largest shrine, the three-storeyed pyramidal **Dharmaraja**, at the southern end, is considered the prototype for the great Dravidian temples. Its sculpture is superb. Some 50 figures include not only gods and heroes, but fascinating, more modest subjects such as temple-servants.

Of the rock-carvings north of the *rathas*, the most celebrated is **The Great Penance**. The narrative sculpture panels cover an entire cliff-face over 24 metres (78 ft.) long and 9 metres (30 ft.) high. A natural split in the rock has been assimilated to the Ganga river descending through the hair of Shiva in the Himalayas, witnessed by gods, heroes and elephants. An ascetic, his ribs jutting out from fasting, balances on one leg.

The **Shore Temple**, bravely withstanding the wind and the waves for 12 centuries (now with a little restorative help from the archaeologists) is masonry-built, comprising two shrines. Shiva the Destroyer faces the dangers out at sea while Vishnu the Preserver watches over the town. The temple is clearly inspired by the monolithic Dharmaraja shrine, but more tapering because originally it had to double as a lighthouse, with a beacon burning at the apex.

Kanchipuram

Kanchi, the "Golden City", has literally scores of temples, hundreds if you include every shrine, dedicated to both Vishnu and Shiva. It is revered as one of the seven holy cities of ancient India* and is a fairly easy trip from Mahabalipuram on your way back to Madras.

*The others are: Varanasi, Mathura, Ujjain, Hardwar, Dwarka and Ayodhya.

You can also plan some relaxing shopping for the much-prized Kanchipuram silk.

Kailasanatha is one of the most important Shiva sanctuaries, dating back to the 8th century. The sandstone temple on a granite base has some graceful sculptures in an inner court of Shiva and Parvati as a celestial king and queen receiving homage from their subjects, at their home on Mount Kailasa.

Vaikuntaperumal is a Vishnu temple of the same period, famous for its elevated colonnade of lively sculpted reliefs narrating the exploits of the Pallava kings.

Pondicherry

The most visible Gallic touch left in this bastion of the French colonial adventure in India is the scarlet *képi* worn by the white-uniformed traffic police waving you on as you drive into town.

Many of the street-names are still French—Rue Suffren (commander of the French fleet here in the 1780s), Rue Lauriston (Napoleon's *aide de camp* born here in 1768) and Rue Dumas (Alexandre)—but Rue Dupleix (France's greatest soldier in India) has become Rue Jawaharlal Nehru. Very few people speak French any more. The French War Memorial on the coast road stands opposite a monument to Gandhi, apostle of non-violence.

After 250 years of French rule

Kanchipuram is equally proud of its temples and superlative silk.

in Pondicherry, the Indians were fortunate to have the great decolonizer, Pierre Mendès-France, to deal with when the time came to retrieve it in 1954.

Apart from the pleasant white sandy **beach**, for nostalgics of the 1960s there's a bitter-sweet pilgrimage to be made to one of that

decade's inspirational Meccas —**Auroville**. This ashram or spiritual retreat was started in 1968 by a French disciple of the internationalist self-help teachings of the Indian sage, Sri Aurobindo. It has lost some of its dynamism with the squabbles following the death of the founder, known just as The Mother. She provided the spiritual and intellectual drive behind experiments in agriculture, textiles and electronics.

But the bold "organic" forms of the community's buildings, with names like Hope, Fraternity and Aspiration, 10 kilometres (6 mi.) north of Pondicherry, still have a striking impact on the landscape. As the cheerful Scandinavians and Bavarians cycle by, 1968 seems as remote as the day the first pale-faced cattle-herders arrived on the other side of India, 3,500 years ago. The Dravidians were already there to meet them.

WHAT TO DO

Sports

What the Indians enjoyed most about the British and vice versa was their enthusiasm for sport. Among their many contributions to Indian civilization, the British brought hockey and cricket. In exchange, they learned the virile delights of polo—imported with the Mughals from Persia and Afghanistan—and the kind of game-hunting that made their grouse shoots on the Scottish moors seem very tame indeed (fox-hunters had to switch to jackals).

Today, with the exception of game-hunting, which has been greatly restricted to protect endangered species, the sporting life in India is still very active. Just be

careful to adapt yourself to the climate and remember that not even mad dogs or Englishmen go out in the midday sun any more. Delhi has excellent modern facilities since staging the Asian Games in 1982.

After all that sightseeing, cool off on a Goa beach.

Participant Sports

Swimming is a natural first choice. Many first-class hotels in the major cities have swimming pools. But, without being paranoid, there are a few precautions you should take elsewhere. Avoid swimming in rivers, ponds, lakes and reservoirs—your body is unlikely to be equipped to deal with some of the other things swimming in there with you.

Beach swimming is best at the recognized resorts rather than the big port-cities, Bombay's Juhu and Chowpatty beaches, for instance, being definitely not a good idea, and though Madras's Marina beaches are much cleaner, there may be sharks. The best resort beaches are on the Malabar coast at Kovalam, Goa and, small but charming, Cochin. Kovalam also has **surfing**, but be careful of the strong currents. On the east coast, try Puri, south of Calcutta, or Pondicherry.

Sailing is possible at most of the resorts. In Madras, you can rent a catamaran and if you're staying at the Taj in Bombay, you should be able to wangle a guest-membership at the nearby Yacht Club.

Fishing is almost exclusively a freshwater proposition, but a very good one. The indigenous mahseer, a distant relative of the carp which can weigh up to around 20 kilos (44 lbs.), is considered as good a sporting challenge as the salmon.

193

The best fishing is up in Kashmir. The streams here were long ago stocked with brown trout from Scotland. Get information and a permit from the Directory of Fisheries in the tourist office building in Srinagar. Consult the tourist office in Delhi for fishing in the Yamuna river and in Bangalore for Karnataka's Cauvery river.

Hiking or **trekking**, as it is more often called here, is a marvellous way of getting away from the often very madding crowd in India and is well organized in the old hill stations. Travel agencies will provide camping and cooking equipment, guides, cooks and even porters, as well as a jeep to

Cricket is more than a passion in India, it's a crazy obsession.

get to the more inaccessible areas.

Once again, Kashmir is a choice region, but you should also try Simla, Darjeeling, Sikkim and, closer to Delhi, the Naini Tal region. This can be improvised on the spot, but a more ambitious six- or seven-day trek needs advance notice and it's a good idea to book through your own travel agent before you leave home.

Golf and **tennis** are readily available in the major cities. Golfers can get guest-memberships in the numerous clubs that the Indians happily inherited from the British and you'll find tennis courts in the big hotels or in public parks.

Many of these hotels also provide a health-club with a **gym** or **yoga** class, the real thing.

Spectator Sports

The most beloved sport in India by far, is **cricket**. There's something in the intricacy of its arcane rules, the controlled passion, even sublimated violence of its action—and perhaps the Brahmanic white uniforms, too—that appeals to the Indian mentality.

It's an astounding obsession—just look at those men and boys walking around streets and airport-lounges with little transistor radios clasped to their ears, praying to Shiva or Vishnu, but more often to murderous Durga or Kali, that India will annihilate its opponent, optimally Pakistan.

All the major cities have attractive stadiums, but for the most fervent atmosphere, try to see a match at the Calcutta Cricket Club (founded in 1792, only five years after the game's holy of holies, the Marylebone Cricket Club in London). If Bengali spirit is too much for you, Brabourne Stadium in Bombay is more relaxed.

Even if you don't get to see a major game or test match (they last five days), you're bound to come across a pick-up game in a back alley of Calcutta or a meadow in Kashmir (where they make the cricket-bats out of the local willow).

Hockey is a British import at which the Indians have surpassed their former masters at the international level and which they have made a much more popular game than it is in Britain. It's played with lightning speed and dexterity by the Indians, who regularly share the Olympic finals with their arch-rivals, Pakistan.

Polo is a speciality of Rajasthan—where the horsemen's jodhpurs originated (see p. 105) —and tournaments are held there, as well as Bombay and Delhi, during the winter months. But it necessarily remains a rich man's sport. Of all the aspects of Indian culture they encountered, this was what British army officers liked most. Some used polo to improve their pig-sticking, while others used pig-sticking to improve their polo.

Horse-racing has a more popular appeal, while paying constant homage to the British with such races as the Calcutta Derby, St. Leger and the Oaks on the Maidan near the Victoria Memorial, or similar races at the lovely Malaxmi race course in Bombay. The highest race course in the country is at Darjeeling. **Camel-racing** is a big thing at Jaisalmer in February and at the autumn festival at Pushkar (see p. 200).

Entertainment

One of the many pleasant surprises in India is the way that its classical **music**, heard perhaps in snatches back in the West and dismissed as something hopelessly beyond an ordinary Westerner's appreciation, grows on you when you hear it in the country of its creation.

To make things easier, rather than what might have been the intimidating atmosphere of a recital-hall, your first encounter with Indian music is likely to be in the pleasant surroundings of a restaurant in one of the smarter hotels. It is often performed as accompaniment to an elegant dinner, with first-class musicians.

In this way, it takes its hold on you imperceptibly, alternately soothing, stimulating, lulling, fascinating, and before you know what, you're hooked, the charac-teristic experience of Indian music.

It consists of two basic elements, the *raga*, a melody of five or more notes, and the *tala*, the rhythm or tempo. Improvisation is of the essence. In a prelude or *alap* which in full-length recitals can last over half an hour, the lead musician seems to grope around until the theme and its infinite variations take hold and patterns emerge from the apparent confusion.

Like the musicians themselves, give yourself up to the hypnotic effect of the notes, rhythms, melodies, even silences. A fully realized performance could go on for another two or three hours (understandably shorter in the restaurant recitals). It is perfectly normal at a concert for people to walk around, fidget and talk at the beginning of the recital until the music asserts itself.

Apart from the big cities and the sophisticated music of the Brahmanic tradition, you can hear the moving folk-music of Rajasthan, rousing or plaintive, positively heart-rending in one of those abandoned villages in the desert around Jaisalmer.

Song, following the same use of rhythm and melody as instrumental music, is both religious and

Kathakali dancers in the South take hours to put on that make-up.

Sitar and Company

Indian music is played not by an orchestra, but usually by just two or three instrumentalists, sitting cross-legged. One of the principal instruments, made famous in the West by Ravi Shankar, is the long six-stringed sitar with its bulbous sound-box. The robust sarangi is played with a bow, joined in the past couple of centuries by the Western violin, but played vertically, with its base held by the musician's bare right foot. The accompanist's four-stringed tambura provides the music's resonant ambience.

The ancient vina, a seven-stringed lute with a rounded body at the base and highly coloured bowl at the top, was played by the goddess Sarasvati, muse of the arts and, like the piano in the West, is played at home by respectable young ladies. The flute you'll see is essentially the same as the one used by Krishna.

There are two kinds of percussion: the small twin drums of the north Indian tabla and the long bulging mridangam drum of south India, held horizontally, with the right hand providing a high-pitched tone for the melody and the left hand beating a deeper tone for the rhythm.

romantic in content. South Indian song is heavy with emotion, both joyful and melancholy, evoked with formidable vocal acrobatics. In the north, where singing was subject to Arabian and Persian influences, it varies between the form known as *dhrupad*, austere, without any embellishment, and the florid *khyal* (India's lyrical equivalent of Neapolitan *bel canto*) or *thumri*, more light-hearted, tender love songs.

In addition to the "dinner-music", the major hotels organize full-scale recitals of music, song and dance, but if you do acquire the taste, look out for concerts in town—Delhi has a lot of recitals around Republic Day at the end of January.

Indian **dance** is marvellously expressive, every hand-gesture, roll of the eyes and movement of shoulder, hip and thigh signifying a whole vocabulary of emotions. Like the intricate sculptures on the temples, the eloquence of dance served as a means of transmitting the message of the sacred scriptures and adventures of the great Hindu epics.

The classical sacred dance, *bharata natyam*, has 108 consecrated forms—you can see them performed by Shiva, in the sculpted frieze of Thanjavur's Brihadisvara Temple (see p. 186). Originally, the dances were performed by *devadasis*, sacred dancing-girls. They were also temple-prostitutes until Hinduism's reform movement of the 19th century made it acceptable for girls of respectable families to perform the dances, too.

In Kerala, try to see the lively *kathakali* dances, in which men play both male and female parts to enact the divine and heroic legends in gorgeous costumes and elaborate make-up. (Performances are regularly held in Cochin's neighbouring town of Ernakulam.) The more sophisticated dance of eastern India is known as *odissi*.

Film in India, produced mainly in Madras, Bombay, Calcutta and Bangalore, is a major industry, if only rarely an art, but the entertainment films are a phenomenon well worth seeing at least once. You may be baffled by the appeal of the musical comedies and violent shoot-em-ups (more than in the West?), but the extravagant melodramas and romantic adventure stories of the historic past have considerable curiosity value for a rainy afternoon. You can learn a lot by what makes Indians cheer, laugh or weep.

Calcutta seems to be the only production-centre with pretensions to artistic creativity, but you're more likely to see the works of Satyajit Ray or Mrinal Sen in Europe or North America than in India itself.

Festivals and Fairs

You could probably spend your whole time in India going to festivals. In a country with such a strong and varied religious tradition and a vital need to have a good time, there's always some reason for celebrating something with a parade. The festivals and fairs bring together fakirs and fortune-tellers, snake-dancers and charlatans. Want to buy a used camel?

Here are a selection (the dates are uncertain because they follow a lunar calendar):

January: *Pongal,* in Trichy and Madurai; a three-day harvest festival during which cows and bullocks are fed with freshly harvested rice. The atmosphere is generally jolly, but the highlight is a variation on the universal bullfight in which young men try to pluck rupee notes that have been spiked on the horns of a very angry bull.

January 26: *Republic Day,* Delhi; great march-past in which India shows off its cultural diversity and military might, the latter nicely softened by a helicopter flying overhead disguised as a flying elephant with the pilot dropping rose-petals on the crowd.

January/February: *Vasant Panchami,* throughout India but best in Calcutta; honouring Sarasvati, goddess of scholars and artists. Everyone dresses up in bright yellow and flies kites.

January/February: *Desert Festival,* Jaisalmer; a celebration of Rajas-thani music and dance, plus camel-races in the local stadium.

February/March: *Mardi Gras,* Goa; the Catholic carnival, a hint of Portugal mixed with a home-grown sweet-smelling whiff of India. Costumes and masks and dancing in the streets.

February/March: *Shivratri,* Khajuraho and Varanasi; a solemn celebration of Shiva, with all-night music and prayers in the temples.

February/March: *Holi,* northern India, best at Mathura, south of Delhi; the spring festival when lovers (and others) spray each other with coloured powder and water.

March/April: *Gangaur,* Udaipur and Jaipur; very colourful procession of girls balancing on their head four or five brilliantly polished brass pitchers, with which they bathe Shiva's wife Parvati (Gauri). The garlanded deity is then accompanied by Shiva at the head of a parade of horses and elephants.

April/May: *Spring Festival,* Srinagar; Kashmiris bring out their samovars for a big tea party to celebrate the first pink and white almond blossoms, highlighted by mid-April festivities in the Mughal Gardens.

At the Puri Rath Yatra *festival, fanatics have been known to crush themselves to death beneath a wheel of Jaggannath's temple-chariot.*

April/May: *Baisakhi*, all over north India; the Hindus' solar New Year. The Sikhs celebrate the anniversary of Guru Gobind Singh's exhortation to form the *khalsa* ("army of the pure").

July: *Rath Yatra*, Puri; one of the greatest festivals of the year, when the three gigantic temple-chariots of Jaggannath, his brother Balabhadra and sister Subhadra are drawn through the streets (see p. 154).

July/August: *Amarnath Yatra*, Kashmir; during the full moon, thousands of pilgrims make their way from Pahalgam to the cave of Amarnath to Shiva's ice-stalagmite lingam.

September/October: *Dussehra*, Mysore, Delhi and Calcutta; ten days of pageant and pomp in great elephant processions following behind the Maharaja of Mysore's throne. In north India, there are music, dance and drama centring in Delhi on the legendary hero Rama (with fireworks blowing up his demon enemy Ravana), and in Calcutta, on the goddess Durga.

October/November: *Pushkar Fair*; this is Rajasthan's big show—camels, horses and bullocks are brought from all over the state to be sold at the market. The camel races are spectacular and this is a fine place to buy Rajasthani craftwork, especially bangles and necklaces.

October/November: *Divali*, all over India; the gayest of all Indian festivities, a combination of Mardi Gras and Christmas, honouring Lakshmi, goddess of prosperity, except in Bengal, where they honour their bloodthirsty goddess Kali, no less gaily, immersing her in the Hooghly river.

November: *Sonepur Cattle Fair*, near Patna; on the banks of the Ganga, this month-long cattle and elephant market is one of the world's biggest, bringing all the usual colourful eccentrics into town.

December 25: *Christmas*, Bombay and Goa; a more religious observance than in most Western countries.

Variable dates:

Muharram, Lucknow; Moslem mourning for Imam Hussein, grandson of Mohammed, when spectacular illuminated bamboo and paper replicas of the martyr's tomb are paraded through the town.

Id-ul-Fitr, Lucknow, Delhi and Calcutta; mosques are lit up as Moslems celebrate the end of the Ramadan fast.

Decorating a giant Divali *puppet in Goa has all the high jinks of a Western Mardi Gras.*

Shopping

From the Greeks to the Turks and Mughals, from Marco Polo to Mountbatten, all were seduced by India's riches, and it's still a great place to shop.

As in any ancient country, its modernizing plunge into the 20th century has produced its fair share of junk and tawdry tinsel, but the traditional craftwork continues at the highest level. Indian silks, carpets, jewellery, perfumes, brassware and wood-carving are first class, and you have the bonus, rare these days, of dealing with the most charming bunch of merchants in the world—even the scoundrels, *particularly* the scoundrels.

At least half the pleasure is in the bargaining. If you don't want to be fleeced, don't plunge in blindly. Go first to the Government Cottage Industry Emporiums, found in almost every major city. The selection here is not usually as wide as you'll find in the privately run shops and you can't haggle, but it'll give you an idea of the range of goods, quality and, above all, the reasonable price.

Then you're ready for the fray, either in the jostle of the great bazaars such as Delhi's Chandni Chowk or Bombay's Bhuleshwar, or the more sedate ambience of grander shops and showrooms. One street-market you shouldn't miss is Bombay's Chor Bazaar or

Feeling the merchandise before the haggling starts in this Calangute beach-bazaar.

Thieves' Market, an extravagant flea market where, among other things, you'll see Indian motorists buying back spare parts stolen from their cars the night before.

If, on your tours of the big cities, you come across products you like from places you'll be visiting later, such as Rajasthan, Varanasi or Kashmir, wait till you get there—the price and selection may be much better.

Haggling with dapper Gujaratis and bright-eyed Kashmiris can attain the level of high art. Certainly there is real aesthetic pleasure, even if you don't land a bargain, in seeing, at the end of the "combat", the beautiful disarray of silks thrown across a coun-

don't, on the other hand, assume everybody is out to cheat you. It spoils the sport.

Carpets, then, are one of the most attractive purchases you can make. Ever since the Mughal emperor Jahangir took Persian craftsmen up to Kashmir with him on his long summer holidays, the handwoven silk and woollen carpets of Srinagar have been among the best in the world.

The silk gives the carpets their unique sheen. Prices vary according to the proportions of silk and wool and the density of the weave. But don't worry, none of them is cheap. Traditional Persian and original Kashmiri motifs of peacocks and fruit trees, tiger-hunts and Mughal lovers make many of them seem too lovely to walk on. They make superb wall-hangings. And even if you don't feel like mortgaging the house to buy a big one, a tiny bedside rug can do wonders on cold winter mornings.

Cashmere is something Kashmiris can be very touchy about. That "100% cashmere" label you show them on your sweater may provoke a snort of "Scotland!" or, more strangled, "Australia!" Then, like an endearment to a beloved one, they murmur "*pashmina*" and spread before you a shawl of soft, warm wool shorn, they tell you, from the underbelly of wild Himalayan goats. And just when you think you've never

ter or a mound of carpets on the floor. The Kashmiris' mercantile wizardry is at its best on the floating market of their *shikaras*, but you will meet some of them down in the plains, to which, like many other wily birds, they migrate in the winter.

If there's no magic formula for the perfect bargain—each person has his own psychological approach—you can avoid two extremes: don't be too eager, but

touched anything finer, they turn around and whisper "*shahtoosh*", the finest Kashmir wool of all, taken from the throat of the ibex and woven so fine that they can pass a shawl right through a wedding-ring.

These, too, are expensive, but you can get shawls of good quality wool, distinctively embroidered, at more reasonable prices.

Silks have long been basic to a fine Indian lady's wardrobe and make magnificent tunics, blouses, stoles or scarves for a Western outfit.

The question arises whether Western women can wear a *sari* or other traditional Indian costumes. It's, of course, a matter of

Mother knows just what she wants, but her demure daughter hesitates.

personal taste, of how "Indian" a woman feels (or *looks*, since blondes often seem incongruous in a sari). The costume most easily adapted to Western tastes, perhaps because it involves trousers, seems to be a tunic worn over baggy pantaloons with a stole around the shoulders, known as *salwar kameez*, most popular in the north-west, very elegant. Younger people prefer the tight-legged *churidar* trousers.

Three towns are especially famous for their silk: Bangalore, for its classic printed silk; Varanasi, for its rich gold and silver brocades; and Kanchipuram, for its heavy, often brilliantly coloured silk favoured for formal saris. And, not forgetting the men, Kanchipuram produces the best silk ties.

Cottons, beautifully hand-printed or embroidered, are probably the best bargain among India's textiles: table-cloths, napkins, bed-linen—gorgeous spreads and pillow-cases—as well as airy light scarves that make life much more comfortable in the Indian heat. Indian tailors are cheap, good and fast, so you might consider having lightweight shirts and baggy pants made up during your stay.

Three cotton-prints to look out for, particularly in Rajasthan: *bagru*, bold geometric or fish, almond and vine patterns in blue, brown and maroon; *sanganeri*, block printed floral and paisley patterns; and *bandhani*, tie-dye, producing decorative splotches of colour. The motifs with mirror-glass stitched into them, much favoured by Rajasthani ladies of the desert for their long flowing skirts, are known as *cutchhi* or *saurashtra*. The dashing coarse cotton Punjabi *phulkari* shawls come in geometrical patterns in orange, pink, green, red and yellow.

Jewellery is very important to the Indians—not only emeralds, rubies and sapphires, but also the semi-precious stones, turquoise, topaz, amber, garnet and amethyst. The heavy craft jewellery of Rajasthan is much sought after.

The Indian diamond mines produced some of the world's greatest gems, including the Koh-i-nur (Mountain of Light) which ended up in the British crown jewels, having originally served as one of the bird's eyes for the Mughals' fabulous Peacock Throne. Although India's mines were long ago superseded by those of South America and South Africa, the ancient art of cutting and polishing has remained in Gujarat. Bombay is a major centre for importing rough-cuts and selling a much admired "finished product".

Don't buy unless you know what you're doing or have a trusted expert with you. Laymen may be interested to know in passing that diamonds are graded alphabetically from D to X, with only D, E, and F being considered good investment, D being colourless or "river white", J is already "slightly tinted", Q "light yellow" and S to X "yellow".

Quite apart from necklaces, brooches and rings—worn on toes as well as fingers—the essential piece of Indian jewellery is the bangle. Whole stalls in the bazaars are devoted to it, silver and gold if you can afford it, but at any rate metal coils, lacquered wood, glass, plastic, and—best bargain of all—colourful varnished *papier-mâché* from Kashmir. (Kashmiris also make very pretty *papier mâché* trays, boxes, bowls and cocktail-coasters.)

Gold, silver, copper and **brass** each has its own bazaar in the big neighbourhood markets of Delhi, Bombay and Calcutta, the most famous being the Jains' Zaveri Bazaar in Bombay, where antique gold is sold with all the hustle and bustle of a fish market. Slightly closer to the price of fish are the lovely brass vases and candlesticks delicately inlaid with green, red, blue or black enamel (best selection in Varanasi).

Wood carvings vary greatly in quality from the rather unimaginative rosewood elephants or sandalwood camels (for some reason, you can't find a good tiger) to the Kashmiris' meticulously fretted walnut work in the style of the screens ornamenting the Srinagar houseboats.

For **modern painting**, try the galleries around Connaught Place in New Delhi, the Pundole and Chemould Galleries in Bombay and the Academy of Fine Arts in Calcutta. If you come across authentic Mughal or Rajput **miniatures** earlier than the 19th century, you're unlikely to be allowed to take them out of the country. For good copies, take a trusted connoisseur with you when buying.

Cooks will be on the look out for **spices**, which we recommend you buy on your last day if possible—chilli, cardamom, turmeric, ginger, cumin, coriander and nutmeg. Kashmir is the place to find saffron, expensive, but cheaper than abroad. For all other spices, try Delhi's Chandni Chowk, the Crawford Market in Bombay or any good food market. The best places to buy are the government-supervised *Khadi Bhandars*, where you can be sure the spices are not adulterated.

Tea gourmets will go for Darjeeling, since only the very finest Assam teas are worth buying here rather than back home. If Darjeeling is on your itinerary, you can buy directly from the plantations or at the town bazaar. (The Darjeeling you buy at home has very often been blended with lesser teas.) When you're buying a couple of kilos, they'll ship it for you in air-tight packages.

EATING OUT

The finest of India's cuisine is as rich and diverse as its civilization and, since Indians don't go out much to restaurants, home-cooking is considered best of all. This is not something you'll be able to sample very often on a first visit, but the major hotels and the few first-class restaurants in the big cities will give you plenty of opportunities to taste the regional variations.

Yes, the food is highly seasoned. Although the spices are much more subtle than just peppery, it will take some time for your stomach to get used to it, even if you're familiar with Indian cuisine back home.

Although the hotels make an effort not to overdo the hotter spices, it's still likely to be sharper than you're accustomed to. So, as with all things in this challenging country, take it easy, a little at a time.

You mustn't expect every day to be a culinary adventure. Unless your tastes are very simple, you may be quickly bored by the food in the more modest establishments and smaller towns.

On the other hand, it would be silly to steer away completely from the local food. It's unlikely that you came all the way to India to eat the same meals you're used to back home. In any case, Indians are much better at cook-

209

ing Indian food than what the menu usually calls—another British legacy that is meaningless in the Asian context—"Continental", i.e. any bland all-purpose Western meals. Only a few hotels break the beef taboo to serve steaks or hamburgers, though even they may be buffalo meat. While you'll inevitably plump for an even mediocre Western meal occasionally, the best way to make a change is to "go Chinese", something the Indians do much better than "Continental".

Breakfast

This is one meal that you may feel happier eating Western-style. All the trimmings of British, if not American breakfasts are usually available: porridge (oatmeal), cereals, eggs and bacon, with the bonus of tropical fresh fruits such as pineapple, papaya and mango, when in season, and their juices.

Coffee in north India is usually instant, but it's worth asking for the excellent Madras brew wherever it's available. Tea is only rarely Darjeeling, but the Assam is as good as any you'd get in British hotels. For safety's sake, the milk is boiled (and re-cooled for the cereals).

Indian-style breakfasts may be rice and curried vegetables, with a drink of *lassi*, a cold liquid yoghurt, sweet or seasoned with salt or cumin. In the south, you'll find *idli*, *dosa* and *hoppers*, different forms of rice- and lentil-flour pancakes which may be folded over mildly spicy vegetables, like an omelette, and served with fruit chutneys.

Scooping up your own spicy mixture is a delicate art.

Lunch and Dinner

If you have plenty to do in the afternoon, keep your lunch light and plan your gastronomic adventure for the evening, around 8 p.m., to give yourself plenty of time to digest it.

The hotels often provide large buffets, giving you a chance to try several dishes, which people tend to pile up on one plate around a mound of rice. But traditional Indian meals, as they are served at home and in the more authentic restaurants, are presented on a *thali*, a large metal platter, with each dish in its separate little bowl, *katori*, so that you can savour the different tastes separately.

Places that have assimilated the British custom will serve a soup first, the famous *mulligatawny* being a spicy chicken, mutton or

vegetable broth concocted for colonial officials. Otherwise, except
at great banquets, the meal is not
divided into courses, everything
usually arriving on your *thali* at
the same time.

You'll find it a good idea to
follow the Indian custom of
drinking before or after, but not
during a meal. Drinking does not
in the end counter a too peppery
flavour because it leaves the taste-
buds defenceless against the next

*The utensils and primus stove are
modern, but the* chapati *recipe is as
old as India.*

hot mouthful. It's better to eat
some plain rice, one of the soft
Indian breads, fruit or, best of all,
yoghurt.

Traditionally, Indians eat, very
nimbly, with their fingers. It is
not a difficult skill to acquire,

212

rotating the finger tips in an elegant motion around the dish to form the food into a ball with rice or Indian bread. Cutlery is, of course, provided, but a fork is not necessarily more hygienic than your fingers.

"Curry"

Properly speaking, there's no such thing. It's a British term invented to refer indiscriminately to India's spicy preparations of fish, meat and vegetables. It has been traced to the Tamil word *kari*, meaning quite simply "sauce".

In India, there is no one "curry powder" or "curry sauce", since each dish requires a different combination of spices, with even more variations than there are French or Italian sauces.

The combination of spices is known as *masala*, mixing, among other things, hot red chilli, coriander, cumin, yellow turmeric and ginger, frequently together with garlic and onions. The other basic seasoning combination, to add richness to a meat sauce (but not usually for fish or vegetables), is *garam masala*, a mixture of cloves, cinnamon, cardamom and sometimes nutmeg and mace. Saffron adds its own unique colour and fragrance, both to rice and to meat. In fine establishments, it's even used to perfume the dining room before the meal begins.

Non-Vegetarian

The classical cuisine of north India, *mughlai*, comes, as its name suggests, from the Mughals, combining Persian and Afghan with Rajput traditions.

With beef taboo for Hindus and pork for Moslems, the most common meat is lamb or mutton, its classic "curry" being *rogan josh*. The cubes of meat are prepared in a yoghurt sauce seasoned with chilli, ginger, coriander and turmeric and an aromatic *garam masala*. This dish originated in Kashmir, where they prepare lamb in dozens of different ways (many of them presented together

---

The Spice of Life

You may be pleased to know that, according to the ancient canons of Indian medicine, the myriad spices concealed in your meal are all working to improve your health. While the general combination stimulates the appetite and helps your digestion in this very special climate, some of the individual spices have some surprising properties.

Turmeric is very good for skin ailments, ginger for your liver or rheumatism. Cloves help the kidneys, relieve fever and stimulate the heart. Coriander fights constipation and insomnia. But one of the most versatile is cardamom, battling bad breath, headaches, coughs and haemorrhoids.

at the same meal if you're lucky enough to attend a *wazwan* banquet, which is traditionally 16, 36 or even 52 dishes!)

Other lamb dishes are the *kebab*, barbecued balls of lamb minced with almonds, pistachios and spices, *tabakmas*, mutton ribs barbecued with a crispy skin, and the royal *goshtaba*, the tenderest lamb taken from the breast, with every last sinew beaten out of it before it is minced into a fragrant dumpling stewed in yoghurt. In Kashmir it is frequently the climactic dish of a wedding banquet (after eating the liver, the kidneys, the shoulder, the leg, and various minced kebabs).

Biriani is a Mughlai speciality which originally was exclusively a lamb dish, though chicken, fish and vegetables are now commonly cooked in the same way.

This festive dish is more elaborate than the *pulao*, which is a simple mixture of rice with lightly flavoured meat or vegetable. *Biriani* entails cooking chicken or cubes of lamb in a sauce of ginger, cardamom, cinammon and cloves before steaming it in the pan with saffron rice and *ghee* (clarified butter). It will often be served decorated with almonds and mint and with an airy-thin foil of edible silver which adds a touch of decorative luxury to the dish, but nothing to the taste.

Indian chickens tend to be a little scrawny, but they are tasty in a rich *makhni* butter sauce as *murg ilaychi*, marinated in a yoghurt mixture of cardamom, ginger, peppers and saffron, or *murg do pyaza*, with shallots and onions.

Tandoori chicken is a very popular barbecue in north-west frontier style baked in a *tandoor* cylindrical clay oven. Typically, the chicken is salted and doused in lime juice, perhaps tenderized with green papaya, then marinated in a yoghurt mixture of ginger, garlic, chilli and saffron, before being plunged on a spit into the charcoal-heated oven. Fish and giant prawns, marinated in different sauces, also make very good *tandoori* dishes.

Rice and Chapatis
The best rice is the aromatic long-grained *basmati*, the common or garden variety being known as *Patna*.

But apart from *biriani* and *pulao*, north Indians do not traditionally include as much rice in their dishes as southerners. They generally prefer to eat their food with a large variety of breads, including a floppy thin *roti* or *chapati*, a slightly thicker *paratha*, sometimes stuffed with vegetables or minced meat, small deep-fried *puri* or giant puffed up *nan*, baked in a *tandoor*. (Before you tackle the rice dishes of the south, try eating with your fingers in the north, folding a piece of *roti* around each morsel.)

Vegetarian
Favourite vegetable dishes are *aloo gobi* (cauliflower and potato), *bharta* (curried eggplant), *sag panir* (spinach with cottage-cheese) and *sabzi bhindi* (lady's fingers with cumin, peppers and onions). These are served with chickpeas or that great staple of any vegetarian *thali* platter, a bowl of *dal*, a thick, subtly spiced porridgy mixture of protein-rich lentils, which come round or flat, mostly yellow or red.

In addition to using more seafood, especially in Goa, the cuisine of south India is much more vegetarian than in the north. This is due to economic reasons of just not having the meat available, but also because the region was not subject to the Mughal influence.

Whereas the north cooks with the products of its cattle, such as *ghee* for frying, yoghurt for sauces and milk for desserts, the basis of southern cooking is the *coconut* —its oil for frying, and the milk and flesh for sauces. This tends to give the food a slightly sweeter taste. Sauces, adding water, vinegar or coconut milk to the spices, are more liquid, gradually ab-

---

Very Fishy
The strictest vegetarians exclude fish, meat, poultry and eggs, even blood-coloured vegetables such as beetroot or tomato, quoting the ancient Sanskrit verse: "In the next world, the animals will eat those who eat them in this world." Some Brahmans of Bengal get around their partiality to fish by calling them "fruit of the sea".

The trouble with those delicious buffets is knowing when to stop.

sorbed by the rice as the meal progresses.

Side-dishes and Snacks

Salads don't exist in the Western sense, but *cachumbar* is a very refreshing side-dish of tomato and onion seasoned in lemon juice or vinegar. The great palate-cooler, north and south, for vegetarian or carnivore, is *raita*, a mixture of cold yoghurt with cucumber, tomato or even pineapple.

As a sweet condiment, not only mango, but mint, coconut, fresh ginger, tomato, dates or tamarind may serve as a chutney (or more properly *chatni*), some of them with an astonishing double punch of sweet and sharp.

There are some very tangy

Desserts

Most desserts betray the excessively sweet tooth of the Mughals. *Ras malai* are patties of cottage cheese and ground pistachio nuts sweetened with syrup and perfumed with rose water and cardamom.

Khir is India's gift to the world's school canteens—rice pudding. Yes, folks, it was invented here—made with condensed milk and broken rice, but much superior to the school version when flavoured with cardamom and nuts. *Gajar halwa*, a dessert of grated carrots stewed in milk and syrup, is best served hot, with raisins and nuts, very pretty. The most interesting ice cream is *kulfi*, made with cardamom and pistachio. There are many kinds of *barfi* and *halwa*, sweets made with flour or milk and flavoured with cardamoms and nuts.

Drinks

The most cooling drinks are *nimbu pani* (fresh lime) or the fruit juices, especially Kashmiri apple. Indian beers are acceptable, white wines drinkable and whisky tolerable. European wines are exorbitant and frankly not a good thing to drink with curry anyway. Among traditional Indian alcoholic drinks are palm toddy in Kerala, rice beer in the Himalayan foothills, *asha*, a meat-based (!) liqueur in Rajasthan and *feni* (cashew-based) in Goa.

snacks. Bombay's best is the *bhelpuri* sold on Chowpatty Beach (see p. 128), a pasty stuffed with fried lentils and chickpeas, noodles, herbs and chutney. The *samosa* is stuffed with meat or vegetables and *pakora* is a vegetable fritter. You have to be careful with *pani puri*, it's a pasty stuffed with tamarind water which squirts all over you if you don't pop the whole thing in your mouth at once.

BERLITZ-INFO

CONTENTS

A ACCOMMODATION

Indian tourist accommodation caters for all tastes. In big cities as well as in all major centres of tourist interest (such as Agra, Jaipur, Srinagar), you will find luxury **hotels**. In former princely states, ancient maharaja's palaces have been converted into hotels; those in Rajasthan are immensely successful. Some have been taken over by large commercial groups, others are still run by members of the princely families. In most cases, however, their popularity has caused a noticeable rise in prices. In old "British India", at slightly cheaper rates, you can find the hotels of yore dear to nostalgics and romantics. Throughout the country there are numerous smaller but comfortable establishments at much lower rates.

If you are not travelling in an organized group or have no reservation, you should head straight for the local tourist office and consult the list of "government approved" hotels. Theoretically, the "government approved" stamp guarantees certain minimal standards in terms of facilities and general hygiene.

If you land up at your destination at a time when tourist offices are closed, you will find, in practically every town, government-run **tourist bungalows**, **hotels**, or **lodges** providing perfectly satisfactory accommodation—rates vary according to the kind of comfort sought (with air-conditioning, hot water, etc.).

Every locality also has a **rest-house** or **dak-bungalow**, which often constitute the best value for money in India (but you may need to bring your own bedding). You should book in advance from the relevant administration's local head office (public works department or the local authorities). Alternatively, you can simply turn up on the doorstep and seek admission and, more often than not, be given a room. It would be pointless, however, to chance to luck in popular tourist centres such as Agra or Jaipur.

Most railway stations have **rest rooms** where you can stay for whole nights, as well as for a few hours. Clean and cheap, they are highly in demand. You must hold a valid railway ticket to qualify for one.

Most establishments will ask you whether you want AC (Air-Conditioned) or Non-AC. From May to September it is wise to spend a few rupees more and enjoy a cool retreat.

Be more than wary of the water in the plastic flask near your bed. Avoid hotels close to cinemas (can be noisy). Water shortages and power cuts (frequent in summer) do not give rise to automatic discounts. In the cheaper hotels, check your bed-linen and do not hesitate to have it changed.

Officially, all foreigners are expected to pay their hotel bills in foreign exchange. This, however, is only really applicable to luxury establishments, since few others have access to the day's rate of exchange.

YMCA and **YWCA hostels** (couples, married or not, are accepted) are in every large town and provide adequate, often excellent, accommodation.

AIRPORTS

Two major international airports, Delhi and Bombay, welcome the bulk of visitors to India. Airports at Calcutta and Madras are also equipped to receive international flights.

Delhi International Airport, Palam, lies about 15 km. (9 mi.) southwest of the city. Terminal facilities include a buffet and restaurant, currency-exchange counters, a post office, luggage deposit, hotel reservation and car-hire counters, and a duty-free shop.

Bombay International Airport is situated 29 km. (18 mi.) north of the city centre. This is by far India's busiest airport, both for international and domestic services. Its international terminal (Sahar), over 5 km. (3 mi.) from the domestic terminal (Santa Cruz) but linked by a regular shuttle-bus service, has all the facilities of a modern airport. At peak hours, the journey from the centre to the airport can take up to one hour, so allow for transfer time.

Arrival (see also CUSTOMS, ENTRY AND EXIT REGULATIONS). On arrival you will be required to fill in a health card (sometimes distributed on board the plane). You will also be asked to fill in a foreign currency form and declare all monies (cash and traveller's cheques) over U.S. $1,000 in value. You then face a choice between a green nothing-to-declare lane, and a red one for those with dutiable items.

Ground transport. Airport terminals provide a cheap bus ride into town at regular timings, throughout the night if the airport is a busy one. Airport bus services exist at most smaller places. You are also assured of finding taxis and motor-rickshaws. Taxi-runs from the airport are on set fares which naturally vary from airport to airport. Convenient pre-paid taxi services operate in Delhi and Bombay. Elsewhere, a policeman at the exit gate will ask for your name and destination: he isn't prying, simply doing his bit to curb taxi-driver greed. You will also be given a complaint card with a telephone number you might want to keep handy. Official taxi fares to various destinations in town are generally posted up near the airport taxi stand.

Departure. On departure, you will be required to pay an airport tax (in rupees). Security checks at airports are particularly intensive.

ALCOHOL

Only one state in India, Mahatma Gandhi's home state of Gujarat, remains completely "dry". Alcohol is generally available elsewhere, except in very remote areas and in religious centres. The once compulsory All India Tourist Permit is therefore no longer necessary. Some hotels, however, will ask you to drink either in your room or in the hotel's licensed bar—up to you to shake off the guilt complex. Other than luxury hotels, few restaurants are authorized to serve beer or other alcoholic drinks. The 1st and 7th of each month are dry days (no alcohol available anywhere) in Delhi, the 1st and 10th in Bombay. The days vary from state to state.

C CIGARETTES, CIGARS AND TOBACCO

Products with Indian brand names are on sale everywhere. Some international companies also manufacture their brands in India. Most people find Indian cigarettes acceptable. Indigenous pipe tobacco and cigars are not always easily available. If you are a compulsive smoker, try the *bidi*, a single leaf of tobacco rolled and filled with shredded tobacco.

The Sikh religion places a ban on smoking so you'll be asked to surrender all your nicotine at the entrance gate when visiting a *gurdwara* (Sikh temple).

CITY TRANSPORT

Taxis exist in all large cities. **Tourist cars** (chauffeur-driven) can be hired out in centres of tourist interest, through the local tourist office.

Other than airport-to-hotel journeys, which operate on a fixed fare basis, drivers must use their meters. Meters, however, are generally out of date, and the driver will show a conversion chart for the fare.

Motor-rickshaws, also known as scooter-rickshaws (three-wheel mini-taxis) operate in a similar way. Again, fare rates vary from town to town; in general, a scooter-rickshaw fare is about half a normal taxi fare. Scooter-rickshaws are banned in Bombay's congested inner city zone, so there it has to be taxi, bus or suburban train.

In all big cities, there is an extremely efficient **bus** service which, once you've learned how to use the bus-route guide available at all bookstalls, may prove very convenient. The only problem is that buses in India carry large crowds.

Other forms of city transport include **cycle-rickshaws** and **tongas** (horse-drawn carts). You agree on the price before starting off. Calcutta and a few other places still have old-style **rickshaws,** pulled by men. Calcutta also has India's first **metro** (subway or underground) line (crowded and hot, but cheap) and India's last operating **tram** service (less crowded, slow and cheap).

CLIMATE (see also pp. 60–63)

India can be conveniently divided into three climatic zones: the north, the south and the hill regions, and into three distinctive seasons: winter, summer and monsoon. The best time to plan your trip to India is from mid-September to early April (except for Kashmir, best from April to September, or the hill stations, good any time in summer except in the monsoon).

Monthly average maximum and minimum daytime temperatures* in degrees Fahrenheit:

		J	F	M	A	M	J	J	A	S	O	N	D
Bombay	max.	83	83	86	89	91	89	85	85	85	89	89	87
	min.	67	67	72	76	80	79	77	76	76	76	73	69
Calcutta	max.	80	84	93	97	96	92	89	89	90	89	84	79
	min.	55	59	69	75	77	79	79	78	78	74	64	55
Delhi	max.	70	75	87	97	105	102	96	93	93	93	84	73
	min.	44	49	58	68	79	83	81	79	75	65	52	46
Madras	max.	85	88	91	95	101	100	96	95	94	90	85	84
	min.	67	68	72	78	82	81	79	78	77	75	72	69

And in degrees Celsius:

Bombay	max.	28	28	30	32	33	32	29	29	29	32	32	31
	min.	19	19	22	24	27	26	25	24	24	24	23	21
Calcutta	max.	27	29	34	36	36	33	32	32	32	32	29	26
	min.	13	15	21	24	25	26	26	26	26	24	18	13
Delhi	max.	21	24	31	36	41	39	36	34	34	34	29	23
	min.	7	9	14	20	26	28	27	26	24	18	11	8
Madras	max.	29	31	33	35	38	38	36	35	34	32	29	29
	min.	19	20	22	26	28	27	26	26	25	24	22	21

*Minimum temperatures are measured just before sunrise, maximum
temperatures in the afternoon.

COMMUNICATIONS (see also Hours)

Telephone and Telegrams. India is in the process of modernizing its
telephone system, raising great hopes for the future. In the mean-
time, however, many city numbers (particularly in Delhi, Bombay
and Madras) are being altered to suit new telephone exchanges.
Before calling, check whether the exchange code (the first two or
three digits in your number) is still correct.

Direct dialling is possible between major cities. Where you make a
call through the operator, you'll have to book a few hours in
advance. There are three basic types of call: *ordinary, urgent* and
lightning. A Delhi-Bombay *lightning* call might take an hour to
materialize (sometimes more) and will cost more than a call of
similar duration from Delhi to New York!

Likewise, the inter-city telegram service is frequently disrupted by
line failure. Public telex is often the best way of reaching a contact in
another part of the country.

Things are much brighter on the international side. Satellite links
can put you through to almost anywhere in the world with a quality
of service up to international standards.

You can book both domestic and international calls through the
hotel switchboard or at the nearest P.T.O. (Post and Telegraph
Office). Big cities will have a 24-hour public telephone and telex
service at the central P.T.O. India has reverse charges (collect)
agreements with most countries, although some hotels will say
otherwise.

Postal Service. The postal service both within India and abroad is
generally very reliable. An airmail letter usually takes up to seven

days to Europe or the U.S. Stamps are sold at post offices and in some large hotels. It is advisable to stand by the post office clerk and watch your letters being franked rather than use public letter boxes. Lower denomination stamps and most envelopes tend not to stick very well, hence the pot of glue on all counters.

You can send some of your bulkier souvenirs home by surface mail, but you must first have the package cleared by customs.

CRIME AND THEFT

One wouldn't really expect to recover a camera left behind on a park bench anywhere in the world; India is no exception to this rule. However, valuables are probably less vulnerable in India than in many parts of the West. Commonsense precautions go a long way to guarantee a safe journey: don't leave valuables lying around, avoid ostentation—a few hundred dollars can mean a year's earnings to many people!

Violence against foreigners is virtually unheard of and it is probably safer to walk the streets of Delhi late at night than in many places back home.

CUSTOMS, ENTRY AND EXIT REGULATIONS

Visas. All travellers to India, including citizens from Commonwealth countries, need visas. There are three kinds of visa: *entry, tourist* and *transit*.

Entry visas apply to those frequently travelling to India on business assignments; they can be extended.

Transit visas have a maximum duration of 15 days and are only necessary if you are merely making a stop-over and want to leave the airport. They are granted to passengers who have tickets for onward destinations. Two-way transit visas can also be obtained.

Tourist visas are normally valid three months and can only be extended at the Government of India's discretion. You must arrive in India within six months of the visa date of issue, or it automatically becomes void.

For a tourist visa, you will need three passport-size photos and, unless you hold a passport from a fee-exempt country, you will be expected to pay for it. Tour organizers can arrange for group visas.

Arrival (see also Airports). Tourists are allowed to bring in all the paraphernalia they normally carry with them. Certain high value items, however, will be entered in your passport by the customs officials. Upon departure, if you are thinking of coming back to

India on the same passport, insist that the customs officers cancel these entries. Items written into passports cannot be sold and have to be shown on departure. In case of loss or theft, you will need to have a police document proving that you have reported the incident.

Fire-arms and habit-forming drugs are banned and so is the import of gold bullion and electronic items for commercial purposes.

Departure. When leaving India, you are allowed to take with you all kinds of souvenirs, provided they are not recognized antiques (over 99 years old)—it is always best to keep your sales receipt with you to appease over-zealous customs officers. You may not export animal skins other than a small amount of cow leather and a few peacock feathers (stay clear especially of tiger-skin rugs and snake skins).

The following chart shows certain duty-free items you may take into India and, when returning, into your own country.

	Cigarettes		Cigars		Tobacco	Liquor	Wine
India	200	or	50	or	250 g.	0.95 l.	
Australia	200	or	250 g.	or	250 g.	1 l. or 1 l.	
Canada	200	and	50	and	900 g.	1.1 l. or 1.1 l.	
Eire	200	or	50	or	250 g.	1 l. and 2 l.	
N. Zealand	200	or	50	or	250 g.	1.1 l. and 4.5 l.	
S. Africa	400	and	50	and	250 g.	1 l. and 2 l.	
U.K.	200	or	50	or	250 g.	1 l. and 2 l.	
U.S.A.	200	and	100	and	*	1 l. and 1 l.	
*A reasonable quantity							

Currency restrictions. It is forbidden to take Indian rupees into or out of the country. There is no limit to the amount of foreign currencies you can bring into India, providing you declare amounts in excess of U.S.$1,000 on arrival. Foreign currencies up to the amount imported and declared may be exported.

E ELECTRIC CURRENT

Electricity supply in all tourist areas and big cities is a standard 220 AC, 50 cycles. Only a few remote parts of northern India are still using DC. During the summer months especially, voltage can fluctuate wildly, so avoid plugging in delicate systems directly without the use of a voltage stabilizer.

Batteries of all types are easily available.

EMBASSIES, HIGH COMMISSIONS AND CONSULATES

Most countries maintain diplomatic ties with India with an embassy or high commission in New Delhi and a consulate in Bombay, Calcutta or Madras.

Australia	*High Commission*: 1/50 Shanti Path, Chanakyapuri, New Delhi 110021; tel. 601400, and 601336/39.
	Consulate: Maker Towers, "E" Block, 16th Floor, Cuffe Parade, Colaba, Bombay 400005; tel. 211071 and 211072.
Canada	*High Commission:* 7/8 Shanti Path, Chanakyapuri, New Delhi 110021; tel. 608161.
	Consulate: (Honorary Consulate only), Hotel Oberoi Towers, Nariman Point, Bombay 400021; tel. 2024343.
New Zealand	25, Golf Links, New Delhi 110003; tel. 697296/318, 697592.
U.K.	*High Commission*: Shanti Path, Chanakyapuri, New Delhi 110021; tel. 601371.
	Consulates: Hong Kong Bank Building, 52/60 Mahatma Gandhi Road, Bombay 400023; tel. 274874/78.
	1 Ho Chi Minh Sarani, Calcutta 700071; tel. 445171, 445175 and 446757.
	24 Anderson Road, Madras 600002; tel. 4731367.
U.S.A.	*Embassy*: Shanti Path, Chanakyapuri, New Delhi 110021; tel. 600651.
	Consulates: Lincoln House, 78 Bhulabhai Desai Road, Bombay 400026; tel. 8223611/18.
	5/1 Ho Chi Minh Sarani, Calcutta 700071; tel. 443611/16.
	Mount Road, Madras 600006; tel. 473040.

GETTING TO INDIA   **G**

Because of the complexity and variability of the many fares, you should ask the advice of an informed travel agent well before your departure.

Scheduled Flights

All major international airlines land at Delhi and Bombay (see under AIRPORTS); some also fly to Calcutta and Madras. Approximate flying times: London–Delhi 11½ hours; New York–Delhi 19 hours.

Charter Flights and Package Tours

From North America: India is extensively featured on a number of tours from the United States, but it is always combined with another country such as Nepal, Sri Lanka, China or Japan. There are no package tours from Canada.

From the United Kingdom: A wide variety of tours is offered, with air/hotel packages to Bombay, Calcutta, Delhi, Goa, Jaipur, Kovalam, Madras and Udaipur. There are also tours available which take in two or more Indian cities, while some combine India with another country such as Nepal or Sri Lanka.

From Australia and New Zealand: India is sometimes featured on Asian tours, but these are not frequent.

Overland

It is possible to cross into India by land from both Nepal and Bangladesh although the journey can be somewhat strenuous (bus from Kathmandu to Dehli; bus from Dhaka to the Bangladesh border, then train to Calcutta. Both routes take a minimum of two or three days). Since the recent turmoil in the western state of Punjab, foreigners are not allowed to travel by land from Pakistan.

H **HEALTH AND MEDICAL CARE** (see also pp. 63–64)

Before travelling to India, you are advised to take out a personal health insurance to cover possible mishaps. Most big insurance companies provide this service.

Likewise, consult your family doctor for a routine check-up and ask him to prescribe medication for potential stomach upsets. Anti-malaria tablets must be taken at least two weeks before departure and for six weeks upon returning home. Remember to pack a small bottle of light wound disinfectant.

Most people during the course of their stay in India will contract some form of stomach trouble. In most cases, it is nothing to worry about, being more of an irritant than anything else. The remedy is simple: avoid rich, spicy food for a while, double-check drinking water (avoid tap water), peel all fruit and take medication if required.

Because of the dramatic weather changes between seasons, people can catch heavy colds at any time to the year. Carrying tablets that combat flu symptoms will help. During the dry, hot season, the dust may cause conjunctivitis, in which case soothing eye drops will come in handy. Sensitive skins also need to be protected against the sun. Bring insect repellent as well as an anti-irritant for insect bites. Excessive heat might cause outbursts of prickly heat (use talcum powder) and migraines. Swallow plenty of liquids and mineral salts to combat dehydration.

Although India no longer insists on vaccinations for tourists (the sole exception concerns travellers arriving from Latin America, parts of Africa and other areas where there is yellow fever), many Western doctors recommend a gamma-globulin injection against hepatitis. Cholera vaccination may help to set your mind at rest, although now discouraged by the World Health Organization. Smallpox has been eradicated in India for the past decade.

Stay clear of stray mammals, particularly dogs: there is a risk of rabies.

Cities such as Delhi and Bombay have a number of Western-style clinics, your embassy in New Delhi will be able to recommend one. Indian Government hospitals are cheap, although they may not function according to the norms you are used to back home. If you are about to have an injection in India, insist either that the doctor uses a disposable needle or that the sterilization process is done in front of you, for your own peace of mind.

HOURS

All central government offices, except post offices, railways, etc., follow a five-day week, closing on Saturdays and Sundays.

Most **markets** close one day each week; the day varies from place to place. **Shops** generally open at 10 a.m. and close by 8 p.m.; some shut for lunch.

Administrative **offices** (other than central railway and airline offices) only start becoming active by 10.30/11 a.m. and will be devoid of life by 5.30 p.m. (official lunch-break is from 1.30 to 2 p.m.). Station booking-counters open with the first trains.

Banks dealing with foreign currency open from 10 a.m. to 2 p.m. on weekdays, and from 10 a.m. to noon on Saturdays. On Saturdays it may be difficult to change traveller's cheques outside the main cities.

Post offices open at 9.30 a.m., closing at 5.30 p.m. in larger places and 3.30 p.m. elsewhere. Getting there early to avoid the crowds isn't always the best idea—you might have to wait some time for the staff to arrive! In major cities, the main telephone and telex office provides a round-the-clock service.

Museums and **parks** close by 5 or 5.30 p.m. (check which day they close).

Hairdressers in large hotels will take clients into the early evening.

L LANGUAGE (see also USEFUL EXPRESSIONS)
Hindi, based on Sanskrit and akin to many European languages, is the official national language of India, but each state also has its own regional language (one of the 15 listed in the Constitution). English continues to be used alongside Hindi for official purposes.

People in north India generally speak Hindi, while in the south, where the regional languages are from the Dravidian group, you'll find more English spoken.

M MAPS
Good road maps of the Indian subcontinent are published in Europe and the U.S. Indian tourist offices hand out useful, although basic, tourist maps of India, as well as tourist brochures.

Street maps are not always available but your best bet will be the local tourist office or your hotel reception desk. Street maps of big cities, like Delhi and Bombay, can be purchased from newspaper stands but are sometimes a little misleading.

The maps in this book were prepared by Falk-Verlag, Hamburg.

MEETING PEOPLE
All transactions and most social encounters in India begin with the established ritual of exchanging visiting cards.

Like everywhere else, politeness in India is a virtue. You'll quickly find that most Indians go out of their way to be friendly and helpful. A traveller will frequently be asked about his nationality, name, marital status and children, though the limited spread of English tends to restrict the scope of most conversations. It can be a bit tedious to go around like a walking curriculum vitae, but just keep smiling. This curiosity is built on the best of friendly intentions.

No topics of conversation are taboo, providing you don't take up an intransigent or arrogant stand. On the contrary, Indians are extremely eager to explain their country and their beliefs to foreigners.

Indians seldom shake hands when greeting people (other than during the course of official business); instead, you'll soon learn to *namasté* with both hands brought together at face level.

Many Indians are teetotal and/or vegetarian, so if you are inviting someone out for a meal, it is always a good idea to inquire beforehand about tastes.

MONEY MATTERS (see also HOURS)

Currency. The Indian unit of currency is the *rupee* (abbreviated *Rs*), divided into 100 *paise*. There are coins of 1, 2, 3 paise (but you'll never see any), of 5, 10, 20, 25, 50 paise and of 1 and 2 rupees. Banknotes exist in denominations of 1, 2, 5, 10, 20, 50 and 100 rupees.

Indians are rather fussy about the condition of their notes. A shopkeeper often turns down a note because it is very slightly torn at the edge while accepting another one with a great big hole in the middle! There is indeed the (very much mistaken) belief that the Reserve Bank of India has ruled that torn-at-the-edge notes are worthless. You should therefore check your change carefully and refuse frayed and dirty notes. Don't try to mend notes with transparent tape—they are unacceptable in this form.

There is a chronic shortage of small cash and many shopkeepers give out sweets or stamps by way of change. Taxi and motor-rickshaw drivers are also notoriously without adequate change and you might often find yourself having to pay a little more to break a roadside deadlock. When cashing in your foreign exchange in a large bank, ask to have part of your Indian money given to you in small notes. Some banks give (extremely valuable) wads of a hundred notes of Rs1 or 2. Hang on to the bank receipts since these will allow you to cash in your excess rupees on departure. Note that it is a criminal offence to change money on the black market.

Traveller's cheques can be cashed in most banks and in many hotels, though, in the latter case, at a slightly inferior rate. Some shops are also authorized to deal in foreign exchange.

Credit cards and personal cheques. The use and acceptability of credit cards is becoming increasingly widespread in India now. All big hotels and government emporiums recognize them, and so do some shops in Delhi and Bombay. Personal cheques, however, will find few takers, although some foreign banks will help you out providing you can produce a foreign resident in India who will stand as surety.

N NEWSPAPERS AND MAGAZINES

English-language newspapers, national and regional, are widespread throughout the country. There are many English-language news magazines, some of which are absolute musts for those interested in the intricacies of Indian political and social life.

Delhi and Bombay have a weekly *What's On* type of magazine (available from bookstalls) which give opening and closing times for museums and information on current cultural events.

P PACKING

While most things are easily available in large Indian towns, there are certain items you'll be happy to have with you.

Other than essential medicines (see HEALTH AND MEDICAL CARE), think of bringing: a drinking-water bottle; a pocket torch (flash-light); a padlock if you are thinking of staying in cheaper hotels (digital padlocks spare the worry of losing the key) or if you are going to travel a lot on Indian railways; a penknife (but don't board planes with it in your cabin luggage); water-purifying tablets; a money-belt and half a dozen passport size photos of yourself if you are applying for permits to Darjeeling or Sikkim or for a rail pass. A universal plug for wash basins will come in handy more often than you might imagine! If batteries are found in your cabin luggage on board a plane, they will be confiscated.

Aspirin is readily available, but you might like to have your own favourite brand handy. Also, don't forget to pack some sterile cotton wool and adhesive bandages and last, but not least, toilet paper or paper tissues (found only in large Indian towns).

Sewing kits can be useful, but in every hotel there will be somebody to do the job for you; if not, on every pavement there is at least one tailor or one cobbler capable of performing instant miracles for a few rupees.

Take a washing powder or liquid detergent if you are thinking of doing your own laundry, although there will always be a *dhobi* laundry service available.

Pack a cloth hat to protect you against the sun, light cotton clothes during the hot and monsoon seasons, a swimsuit, and a pullover during the winter months or if you are going to the hills (see also CLIMATE).

When travelling long distances by rail, a bed-sheet can make a lot of difference to your comfort and so will a plastic or aluminium mug (allows you to drink tea, bought on the platform, when the train moves off). Ear plugs can sometimes be a life-saving device, particularly at night in crowded compartments or in a bus with non-stop Indian film music (often distorted) blaring out of the public address system. A short-wave transistor radio will enable you to keep in touch with world affairs.

Finally, you might also like to bring with you a few small gifts for people who have been particularly helpful. Anything with a foreign trademark on it will be happily accepted; disposable gas lighters, ball point and coloured felt-tip pens, stamps from your own country, cigarettes, picture postcards, perfume samples, etc. In many places you might find yourself surrounded by swarms of children clamouring for "school pens, stamps and coins".

PHOTOGRAPHY

Film for slides is not easy to find in India. Some shops in big cities do stock E6 preparations (Agfachrome, Ektachrome, Fujichrome, etc.) but retail prices are about three times what they are in Europe. Colour-print film and black-and-white rolls are more common.

Delhi and Bombay and other larger towns have plenty of photo studios which can process black-and-white or colour film; quality, however, will vary substantially. Better take the film back home with you and have it processed there.

Customs impose a limit of 25 rolls of film per person. Although all metal detector machines are said to be film-safe, you might feel happier, when passing airport security checks, to carry your film in a clear plastic bag you'll hand over to the security staff for inspection.

India is a colourful country and your right hand index finger will be itching on the shutter trigger from the moment you arrive. There are, however, certain things which can't be photographed: military installations, bridges of all sorts, airports and railway stations, power stations and refineries, dams and telephone exchanges. Likewise, it is always best to get permission to photograph anyone. Women in rural areas are often extremely camera-shy.

PLANNING YOUR TRIP

Most of India is open to foreign travel, with the exception of the territories of Assam, Arunachal Pradesh, Nagaland, Manipur, Mizoram, Tripura and Meghalaya. There is also an "inner-line" exclusion zone running along the frontier between India and China. People wishing to trek in Kashmir and Ladakh, as well as parts of Darjeeling and Sikkim, should inquire at the local tourist office before setting off: some hill areas may be completely open, others may need special access permits (see p. 155), and others still can be entirely out of bounds.

F.R.R.O.'s (Foreigners Regional Registration Office) in Delhi, Bombay, Calcutta, Madras amd other state capitals, come under the umbrella responsibility of the Under Secretary, Home Affairs Ministry, Foreigners Division, Lok Nayak Bhavan, Khan Market, New Delhi 110003. They are ultimately in charge of all visa and permit problems.

POLICE

Traffic police do not carry guns; uniforms (on the colourful side) vary from state to state. Police forces responsible for law and order are armed, officers with revolvers and the men with Enfield rifles.

Banks are guarded by armed retired servicemen. Each locality has one or more police stations or police booths where foreigners can register complaints.

PRICES

The following are some prices in Indian rupees and U.S. dollars. However, they must be regarded as approximate as inflation is ever present.

Airport departure tax. Rs300 (Rs150 to neighbouring countries).

Car hire. Cost per kilometre between Rs3 and Rs4 for a non-air-conditioned car; Rs5 upwards for an AC Indian car; more for a luxury imported vehicle; Rs20 upwards per hour waiting charges. Overnight charges for the driver (all rented cars are chauffeur-driven) start from Rs100 per night.

Cigarettes from Rs9 to Rs25 for a packet of 20.

Discover India Pass. 21 days U.S.$375.

Hairdresser. From Rs20 for a man's haircut in a luxury hotel; from Rs70 for a woman's shampoo and cut.

Hotels. Double room in a luxury establishment between Rs1,400 and Rs2,200 per night. Middle of the range hotels from Rs1,000 to Rs1,700 per night for a double, depending on whether air-conditioned or not. Local and luxury taxes (a few per cent, approximately 3 to 15, depending on the state) extra.

India Wonder Fare. 21 days U.S.$400.

Indrail Pass. First Class U.S.$110 for 7 days, U.S.$400 for 90 days (double for air-conditioned class).

Meals. A snack meal (Indian style): Rs20 upwards in a middle-range restaurant; twice that in a luxury hotel. Full meal (Indian style): from Rs50.

Taxis to and from airports are supposed to operate at a fixed rate. **Motor-rickshaws** are allowed to drop passengers at the airport but they are not allowed to pick up there. In other places the motor-rickshaw fare is about Rs1.40 per kilometre; double for taxis.

Trains. Delhi to Bombay (approximately 1,400 kilometres) AC first class Rs1,000, non-AC first class Rs480, AC second class Rs600, non-AC second class Rs140, AC chair car Rs280.

PUBLIC HOLIDAYS

Because of the multiplicity of religions, holidays are plentiful and confusing.

Fixed national holidays are: January 26, Republic Day; May 1, Labour Day; June 30, half-yearly closing on bank accounts (banks only); August 15, Independence Day; October 2, Mahatma Gandhi's Birthday.

Other holidays vary according to region.

A list of official holidays can be obtained from tourist offices.

RADIO AND TV

All India Radio (A.I.R.) broadcasts on medium wave, with news in English, Hindi or a regional language.

Indian television consists mainly of song and dance shows, Indian films, indigenous and imported soap-operas, information for farmers and science and general interest programmes. News is given in Hindi and English (at 9 p.m. and 10 p.m. respectively). Luxury hotels generally provide a TV set in each room.

RELIGIOUS SERVICES

No other country in the world has such a wealth of faiths as India. Access to places of worship is generally open, except for some Hindu temples and all Parsi fire-temples. Mosques are closed to non-Muslims at certain times of day. In most places of worship you'll be asked to take off your shoes and/or cover your head. Sikh *gurdwaras* ban the entry of tobacco, while Jain temples forbid all forms of animal leather (including wallets).

Synagogues can be found in big cities such as Bombay and Delhi, Christian churches of all kinds exist in practically every town.

RESTAURANTS (see also p. 209)

First-class hotels naturally offer sophisticated surroundings and a touch of luxury for the traveller. You will nearly always find middle-range restaurants (for both Indian and Chinese food) where quality of food and service will vary between good and mediocre; there is no fool-proof way of sorting out the better restaurants before trial.

Many of the small roadside establishments, unenticing by all Western standards of conviviality, sometimes serve excellent fare for next to nothing, but these are not recommended for the short-stay traveller.

On the Menu

aloo	potato
barfi	sugar and milk sweets
biriani	north Indian rice and meat dish
chai	tea
chapati	unleavened bread, cooked on an open pan or griddle
chawal	rice
dal	lentils or kidney beans
faluda	sweet noodles with milk and ice cream
gosht	meat, generally mutton
halwa	carrot-based or semolina dessert
idli	little dumpling of steamed rice flour, eaten at breakfast with chutney and curry
kebab	barbecued meat
keema	minced meat, generally mutton
kirra	cucumber
kofta	spicy minced-meat balls
korma	a curd-based curry sauce
kulfi	Indian ice-cream
lassi	curd-based milk-shake, sweet or salty
masala	mixed spices
masala dosa	pancake of rice flour and ground lentils with spicy potato filling
mutter	peas
nan	leavened bread
nimbu pani or *nimbu soda*	fresh lime with water or preferably soda

pakora	deep-fried savoury fritter with onion or potato
paneer	Indian cottage cheese
papad/papadum	crispy spicy wafers
paratha	flaky *chapati*, generally fried in butter and often stuffed
pomfret	type of very fleshy fish
pulao	north Indian rice and meat dish
puri	deep-fried "bubble" *chapati*
raita	curd (*dahi*) mixed with tomato, green peppers or cucumber
roomali roti	paper-thin *chapati* ("roomal" means handkerchief)
roti	generic name for oven- or pan-cooked bread
sabzi	vegetables
sag	a type of spinach
samosa	deep-fried stuffed pasties
seer	type of very fleshy fish
tandoori	meat (generally chicken) marinated in spice and curd, cooked in a traditional oven
tikka	pieces of diced meat/fish, marinated and grilled on an open fire

TIME DIFFERENCES   T

Indian Standard Time (IST) is GMT plus 5½ hours, winter and summer alike. The most bizarre time difference in the world exists between India and Nepal: 10 minutes!

	New York	London	**Delhi**	Sydney
January	1.30 a.m.	6.30 a.m.	**noon**	5.30 p.m.
July	2.30 a.m.	7.30 a.m.	**noon**	4.30 p.m.

TIPPING

It is customary to leave a tip of about 10% of the total bill in restaurants. Elsewhere, tipping is discouraged by the Government of India. Do not try to tip government employees, although museum guides will invariably give hints at the end of a conducted tour! In temples, however, the *baksheesh* is more or less mandatory; you should also give a rupee to the person who looked after your shoes while you were visiting.

TOILETS

Generally, very, very basic. Don't shun the "eastern" (seatless) version, they are often much more hygienic than the European style. The water tap (faucet) nearby is to wash afterwards.

Tourists will often bless their stock of paper tissues.

TOURIST INFORMATION OFFICES

Indian Tourist Offices at the following addresses will help prepare your trip:

Australia: 9th floor, Carlton Centre, 55 Elizabeth Street, Sydney, NSW 2000; tel. (02) 232-1600, (02) 232-1796.

Canada: 1016 Royal Trust Tower, Toronto Dominion Centre, P.O. Box 3412 Toronto, Ontario MSK 1K7; tel. 416-362-3188, 416-362-3881, 416-362-3666.

Japan: Pearl Building, No.9-18 Ginza, 7 Chome, Chuo-Ku, Tokyo-104; tel. (03) 571-5062/63.

U.K.: 7 Cork Street, London, W1; tel. 01-437 3677/8.

U.S.A.: 30 Rockefeller Plaza, Room 15, North Mezzanine, New York, N.Y. 10020; tel. (212) 586-4901, (212) 586-4902/3.
230 North Michigan Avenue, Chicago, IL 60601; tel. (312) 236-6899; (312) 236-7869.
3550 Wilshire Boulevard, Suite 204, Los Angeles, CA 90010; tel. (213) 380-8855.

In India the major tourist offices are:

Bombay: 123 M Karve Road; tel. 291585, 293144.
Santa Cruz Airport; tel. 569031.

Calcutta: "Embassy", 4 Shakespeare Sarani; tel. 441475, 443521.
Dum Dum Airport. Tel. 57261/44.

Delhi: 88 Janpath, New Delhi 110001; tel. 3320005.
Indira Gandhi International Airport: international arrival lounge (open 24 hours), tel. 391711; domestic arrival lounge (open 8 a.m. till last flight—around 11 p.m.), tel. 3295296.

Madras: 154 Anna Salai; tel. 88686/5.
Meenambakam Airport; tel 431686.

Generally, airport tourist offices are open 24 hours, and others from 9 a.m. to 2 p.m. only.

TRAVELLING AROUND INDIA (see also p. 64)

Air (see also AIRPORTS). India has an excellent airline network. The only real problem is booking; many of the more popular routes, such as Delhi–Srinagar, are full up months in advance. So don't waste time on arrival: as soon as you know where you are going and how you want to get there, book. There are two types of ticket: *confirmed* which are (generally) trouble-free, and *requested* which frequently only offer a slim chance of travel.

Indian Airlines (IA), the state-owned domestic carrier, offers tourists two discount schemes: a 7-day *India Wonder Fare* (one region only) or a 21-day *Discover India* fare, with unlimited travel, but only one stop in each town. The *Discover India* tickets must be purchased abroad either at Air India offices or at an agreed travel agent. The *India Wonder Fare* can by obtained in India but must be paid for in foreign currency. There is a 25% discount on all full-fare tickets for travellers under the age of 30. Tourists are expected to pay for their tickets in foreign exchange.

In Delhi, the IA office is at Kanchenjunga House, Barakhamba Road, New Delhi 110001; tel. 3310071 and 0052.

In Bombay: Air India Building, Nariman Point, Bombay 400 021; tel. 2024142; 2023747.

India also has a small feeder-service called *Vayudoot* which links up smaller towns, particularly useful if you are thinking of going to some of the more remote hill stations.

Vayudoot head office is at: Malhotra Building, Connaught Place, New Delhi 110001; tel. 3312779.

Rail. Indian Railways (administratively divided into: Northern, Western, Eastern, Central and Southern railways) have five basic classes of travel: First Class Air Conditioned (AC), Second Class AC, AC Chair, First Class non-AC and Second Class non-AC. In the summer months an AC compartment is advisable, especially if travelling through the Indian plains.

Other than a few super-de-luxe fast trains, there are three types of train: *Express, Mail* and *Passenger*. You will certainly avoid *Passenger* trains which stop at every station no matter how long the journey.

Tourists will find the *Indrail Pass* the best buy if they intend to use the train a lot. These are valid for unlimited travel for 7–90 days.

Pass holders have a priority booking allowance at most stations. *Indrail Passes* can be purchased abroad through approved travel agents. You can buy them in India from approved travel agents and at special railway-station booking counters for tourists in Delhi, Bombay, Calcutta, Madras, Goa, Bangalore, Varanasi, Agra, Ahmadabad, Aurangabed, Chandigar, Gorakhpur, Hyderbad, Jaipur, Trivandram, Amritsar, Rameswaran and Vadodara.

All long-distance trains have sleepers. Second-Class non-AC berths are wooden planks; First-Class and AC berths are cushioned. Second-Class berths, whether AC or not, give straight onto the central corridor, whereas First-Class berths are in separate compartments with slide-door and catch-lock.

In First-Class and AC, you can hire sheets and blankets (nights can be chilly in AC even in summer).

Bring plenty of reading material, fruit and drinking water. You will marvel at the ability of Indian travellers to disembark after a 48-hour journey as clean and fresh as when they started, while you will be in dire need of soap and water.

Food is served on Indian trains. Apart from one or two luxury trains, there won't be much of a choice (generally it will simply be a question of vegetarian or non-vegetarian) and will consist of a *thali* or a cardboard box filled with plastic bags of curry and rice.

For booking tickets, foreigners need their passports.

Road. Where there's no railway (e.g. parts of Rajasthan), there'll be a road and on that road there'll be dozens of inter-city buses. The fares, by Western standards are negligible and, generally, so is the comfort! Buses on important routes, like Agra and Srinagar are, on the contrary, plush and classy.

Discovering India by car is by far the best way. Cars are hired chauffeur-driven.

W WEIGHTS AND MEASURES
India uses the metric system everywhere.

Temperature

°C -30 -25 -20 -15 -10 -5 0 5 10 15 20 25 30 35 40 45
°F   -20 -10 0 10 20 30 40 50 60 70 80 90 100 110

Length

| cm | 0 | | 5 | | 10 | | 15 | | 20 | | 25 | | 30 |
| inches | 0 | | 2 | | 4 | | 6 | | 8 | | 10 | | 12 |

| metres | 0 | 1 m | | 2 m |
| ft./yd. | 0 | 1 ft | 1 yd. | 2 yd. |

Weight

| grams | 0 | 100 | 200 | 300 | 400 | 500 | 600 | 700 | 800 | 900 | 1 kg |
| ounces | 0 | 4 | 8 | 12 | 1 lb. | 20 | 24 | 28 | 2 lb. |

Fluid measures

| imp.gals. | 0 | 5 | 10 |

| litres | 0 | 5 | 10 | 20 | 30 | 40 | 50 |

| U.S.gals. | 0 | 5 | 10 |

Kilometres to miles

| km | 0 | 1 | 2 | 3 | 4 | 5 | 6 | 8 | 10 | 12 | 14 | 16 |
| miles | 0 | ½ | 1 | 1½ | 2 | 3 | 4 | 5 | 6 | 7 | 8 | 9 | 10 |

USEFUL EXPRESSIONS

Hindi is spoken mainly in the north. Here are some useful words and expressions. Verbs ending with a "-yé" sound are polite imperatives, those ending with a "-o" are familiar forms of address. The "-ji" suffix is a polite honorific. A wavy line over a vowel indicates a nasal sound.

Yes	ji hã
No	nahĩ
Please	meher bāni
Thank you	dhanyavād (sometimes "shuk-riyā" in northern India)
Beg your pardon/sorry	māf (or shama) kijiyé
Hello/welcome/goodbye	namasté
How are you?	kyā hāl hai/āp kaisé haĩ
I'm fine	thīk hai
I don't understand	samjhā nahĩ

241

Tomorrow/yesterday (confusion is possible)	kal
Today	āj
Tonight	āj rāt ko
This morning	āj subhā
This evening	āj shām ko
Good	achchā
Excellent/well done	shābāsh
Fast/early	jaldi
Slow/late	dhiré
Money	pāisā
How much is it?	kyā dām hai
It is very expensive	yé bahut mahinga hai
Are you free? (taxi, rickshaw)	kyā āp khāli haĩ
How far is it?	kitni dūr hai
Where is it?	kahā hai
On your right	dāy
On your left	bāy
Straight ahead	sidha
Please stop here.	yahā rokiyé
Please go faster.	jaldi chaliyé
Please go slowly.	dhiré chaliyé
Please go away.	jāiyé
Go away!	jāo
Let's go!	chalo (polite form chaliyé)
Please bring	lāiyé
Please take	lijiyé
Please give	dijiyé
I'm not feeling well.	maĩ kuchch bimār hũ
I need a doctor.	mujko doctor chaiyé
This is not good	yé achchā nahĩ hai

It is very good.	bahut achchā hai
It is very hot.	bahut garam hai
It is very cold.	bahut thandā hai
It is very beautiful.	yé bahut sunder hai
Please give me some water.	mujko pani dijiyé
This is not clean.	yé saf nahī hai

NUMBERS

1	ek	12	barah
2	do	20	bis
3	tin	30	tis
4	char	40	chalis
5	panch	50	pachās
6	chhé	60	sāth
7	sat	70	sattar
8	ath	80	assī
9	nau	90	nabbé
10	dass	100	sau
11	gyarah	1,000	hazār

The following two are fairly important since they are not only typically Indian but also occur frequently in the press, on official documents etc.

100,000	lakh (written: 1,00,000)
10,000,000	crore (1,00,00,000)

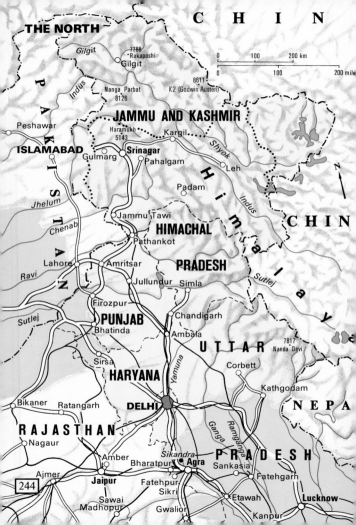

THE NORTH

C H I N A

PAKISTAN

Gilgit
7788
Rakaposhi
Gilgit

0   100   200 km
0   100   200 mil

Nanga Parbat
8126

8611
K2 (Godwin Austen)

Peshawar

JAMMU AND KASHMIR

Haramukh
5143

Kargil

ISLAMABAD

Gulmarg   **Srinagar**

Pahalgam

Shyok

Leh

Indus

C H I N A

Jhelum

Padam

H
i
m
a
l
a
y
a

Jammu Tawi

Chenab

HIMACHAL

Pathankot

Lahore   Amritsar

PRADESH

Jullundur   Simla

Ravi

Sutlej

Firozpur

Sutlej

PUNJAB   Chandigarh

Bhatinda   Ambala

U T T A R

7817
Nanda Devi

Sirsa

HARYANA

Corbett

Bikaner   Ratangarh   **DELHI**

Kathgodam

RAJASTHAN

Ganga

N E P A

Nagaur

Ramganga

P R A D E S H

Amber   *Sikandra*

Bharatpur   **Agra**   Sankasia

Ajmer

Fatehpur   **Jaipur**   Sikri

Sawai   Madhopur   Gwalior

Etawah   Fatehgarh

Lucknow

Kanpur

244

THE EAST

CHINA

BURMA

Bay of Bengal

ARUNACHAL PRADESH
Kundil
Brahma
Bazar
Okund
Namdapha
North Lakhimpur
Itanagar
NAGALAND
Kohima
ASSAM
Dispur
MANIPUR
Imphal
Shillong
MEGHALAYA
Aizawl
MIZORAM
Demagir
TRIPURA
Agartala
Brahmaputra
Dhaka

HIMALAYA
NEPAL
Katmandu
SIKKIM
Timphu
Gangtok
Darjeeling

Brahmaputra
Padma
Ganga
Mouths of the Ganga

Calcutta
Haldia
WEST BENGAL
BIHAR
Jamshedpur
Paradwip
Ranchi
Keonjhargarh
Konorak
Puri
Bhubaneshwar
ORISSA
Sambalpur
Rourkela
Gumla
Saraipali
Udaigiri
Jagdalpur
Vizianagaram
Visakhapatnam

Fatehgarh
Kanpur
Gorakhpur
Lucknow
UTTAR PRADESH
Motihari
Patna
Varanasi
Sarnath
Allahabad
Sasaram
Nalanda
Mokameh
Rajgir
Bodh Gaya
Amarkantak
Khajuraho
Rewa
Katni
Jabalpur
MADHYA PRADESH
Raipur
Kanha
Mahanadi

Motihari

247

N

0   100   200 km
0   100   200 miles

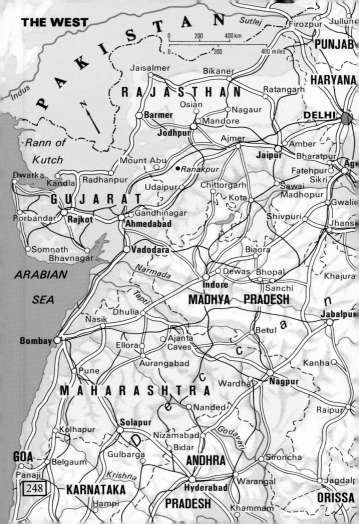

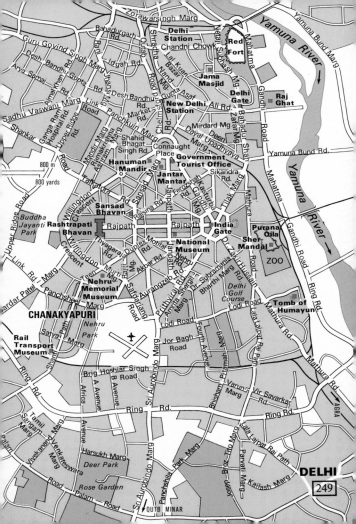

NASIK, INDORE,
WORLI BUDDHIST
TEMPLE

AIRPORT,
SANTA
CRUZ

POONA

Haines Rd.

Prabhu Velley Rd.

Delisle Road

Babasaheb Ambedkar

Reay Road

Bombay Docks

**Dhobi
Ghat**

Clerk
Road

Haines
Road

Victoria and Albert Museum

Victoria
Garden

Zoo

Victoria Rd.

Reay Rd.

Arthur Rd.

Mahim Bay

Haji Ali's Tomb

Clerk

BYCULLA

Love Lane

Mount Rd.

Nesbit Rd.

MAZAGAON

*Elephant
Cave*

**Mahalaxmi
Temple**

Dr. Anandrao Nair Rd.

**Central
Station**

Bellasis Road

Babula Tank Rd.

Wadi Bunder
Rd.

D'Mello Rd.

*Cross
Island*

Carmichael (Warden) Road

Peddar Road

Bhulabhai Desai Rd.

Tardeo Rd.

TARDEO

Falkland Road

Foras Road

Grant Road

Grant Road

Sardar Patel Road

Duncan Rd.

Sardar Patel Rd.

Argyle Road

Masjid Bunder Rd.

D'Mello Rd.

Gowalia Tank Rd.

Hughes Rd.

Girgaum Rd.

Vithalbhai Patel Rd.

GIRGAUM

Mumbadevi Temple

**Towers
of Silence**

*Hanging
Gardens*

Gibbs Rd.

Harvey Rd.

Girgaum Rd.

Hardware Street

Kalbadevi Street

Cotton Exchange

Carnac Rd.

D'Mello Rd.

Crawford Market

*Kamala
Nehru Park*

**Statue
of Tilak**

Queen's Road

Netaji Subhash Road

Aquarium

Queen's Rd.

Carnac Naoroji Rd.

**Victoria
Terminus Station**

Nepean Sea Road

Ridge Road

Walkeshwar Rd.

Cruickshank Rd.

Mahapalika Rd.

Dadabhai Naoroji Rd.

**General
Post Office**

Jain Temple

Marine Drive

New Marine Rd.

Mahatma Gandhi Rd.

**Handloom
House**

FORT

Mole Station

Ballard Rd.

**Walkeshwar
Temple**

B a c k   B a y

**Government of India
Tourist Office**

Churchgate Station
Flora Fountain

**St. Thomas
Cathedral**

Mint

**Town Hall
Central Lib**

**Raj Bhavan,
Government House**

Malabar Point

D'Watcha Rd.

Sachivalaya

Rajabai Tower

*Mayo
Road*

Jehangir Art Gal

**Prince of Wa
Museum**

Statue of Sivaji

Queen's Rd.

Madam Carna Rd.

**Gateway
of India**

N

Cuffe Parade Road

Colaba Rd.

COLABA

ST. JOHN'S CHURC

0   400   800 m

0   400   800 yards

BOMBAY

250